GO FOR DevO

AUTOMATION, ORCHESTRATION, AND CLOUD-NATIVE DEVELOPMENT

HAWKINGS J CROWD

Preface

This book is a practical guide to leveraging the power of Go for modern DevOps practices. In today's rapidly evolving technological landscape, the ability to automate, orchestrate, and secure complex systems is paramount. Go, with its performance, concurrency, and rich standard library, has emerged as a leading language for building the tools and systems that drive DevOps forward.

This book is not just another Go programming tutorial. While we will cover essential Go concepts as they relate to DevOps tasks, the primary focus is on practical application. We aim to equip you with the knowledge and skills to build real-world solutions, from automating infrastructure management with Terraform to building robust CI/CD pipelines and securing cloud-native applications.

We'll journey through the key areas of DevOps, demonstrating how Go can be used to:

Interact with and manage infrastructure using tools like Terraform.

Automate server configuration and system state management.

Build and manage Docker images and orchestrate containers.

Deploy and manage applications on Kubernetes.

Implement comprehensive testing and CI/CD pipelines.

Build monitoring agents and dashboards.

Implement robust security practices throughout the development lifecycle.

Each chapter is designed to be self-contained, providing clear explanations, practical examples, and best practices. We encourage you to not just read but actively engage with the code examples, experiment, and adapt them to your specific needs.

This book is for developers, DevOps engineers, system administrators, and anyone interested in using Go to improve their DevOps workflows. A basic understanding of programming concepts is assumed, but prior experience with Go is not required. We will introduce the necessary Go concepts as we progress.

We believe that Go is a powerful tool for building the future of DevOps, and we are excited to share our knowledge and experience with you. By the end of this book, you will be well-equipped to harness the power of Go to automate, orchestrate, and secure your systems, enabling you to build and deploy applications more efficiently and reliably.

Welcome to the world of Go DevOps! Let's get started.

TABLE OF CONTENTS

Chapter 1

Chapter 2

Chapter 3

Chapter 4

Chapter 5

Chapter 6

Chapter 7

Chapter 8

Chapter 9

Chapter 10

Chapter 1

Getting Started with Go for DevOps

1.1 Setting Up Your Go Environment for DevOps

This chapter lays the foundation for your DevOps journey with Go. We'll walk through setting up your Go environment, ensuring you have the necessary tools and configurations to develop and deploy Go applications effectively. Whether you're a seasoned Gopher or just starting, this chapter will provide a solid starting point.

1. Installing Go:

The first step is installing Go itself. The official Go website (https://go.dev/dl/) is the best place to download the correct distribution for your operating system (Windows, macOS, Linux, etc.). The website provides clear instructions for each platform. Generally, the process involves downloading an archive or installer and following the platform-specific instructions.[1]

Windows: The MSI installer is the recommended approach. It handles setting up the necessary environment variables automatically.

macOS: You can use the `.pkg` installer or, if you prefer a package manager, consider using Homebrew (`brew install go`).

Linux: Download the tarball and extract it to a suitable location (e.g., `/usr/local/go`). You'll then need to add the Go binaries to your system's PATH environment variable.[2] This usually involves adding a line like `export`

`PATH=$PATH:/usr/local/go/bin` to your `.bashrc`, `.zshrc`, or equivalent shell configuration file.

2. Verifying the Installation:

After installation, open a terminal or command prompt and type:

Bash
go version

This command should display the installed Go version (e.g., `go version go1.20 darwin/amd64`). If you see the version information, Go is installed correctly. If you encounter an error, double-check your installation steps and ensure the Go binaries are in your PATH.

3. Setting up the Workspace (GOPATH and Go Modules):

Go uses workspaces to organize your projects.[3] Historically, this was managed using the `GOPATH` environment variable. While `GOPATH` is still supported, the recommended approach for modern Go development is using Go Modules.

Go Modules (Recommended): Go Modules are the default way to manage dependencies in Go 1.11 and later.[4]They eliminate the need for `GOPATH` and provide a more flexible and robust way to manage project dependencies. To enable Go Modules, ensure you are outside of your `GOPATH` when starting a new project, or set the environment variable `GO111MODULE=on`. Create a new directory for your project, navigate into it, and initialize a new module using:

<!-- end list -->

Bash

```
go  mod  init  <your-module-name>      // Example: go  mod  init
github.com/yourusername/yourproject
```

This command creates a `go.mod` file in your project directory, which will list your project's dependencies.

GOPATH (Less Common Now): If you're working with older projects or have a specific reason to use `GOPATH`, you'll need to set the `GOPATH` environment variable to a directory where you want to store your Go projects. Inside the `GOPATH` directory, you'll typically have three subdirectories: `src` (for source code), `bin` (for compiled binaries), and `pkg` (for package objects). You'll also need to add `$GOPATH/bin` to your PATH.

4. Installing Essential Tools:

While Go comes with a powerful standard library, several tools can enhance your DevOps workflow:

Git: Essential for version control.[5] If you don't have it already, install it from your system's package manager or the official Git website (https://git-scm.com/).

Docker: Crucial for containerization, which is a cornerstone of modern DevOps.[6] Download and install Docker Desktop (for Windows and macOS) or Docker Engine (for Linux) from the Docker website (https://www.docker.com/).

Kubernetes (kubectl, minikube): For container orchestration.[7] `kubectl` is the command-line tool for interacting with Kubernetes clusters. `minikube` allows you to run a single-node Kubernetes cluster locally for development and testing. Install these tools according to the Kubernetes documentation (https://kubernetes.io/docs/).

Delve (dlv): A powerful debugger for Go. Install it using: `go install github.com/go-delve/delve/cmd/dlv@latest`

Go linters (golangci-lint): Help enforce coding standards and best practices.[8] Install it using: `go install github.com/golangci/golangci-lint/cmd/golangci-lint@latest`

5. Setting up Your IDE or Text Editor:

Choose an IDE or text editor that suits your preferences. Popular choices for Go development include:

Visual Studio Code (VS Code): A highly popular and versatile editor with excellent Go support via the Go extension.[9]

GoLand: A dedicated IDE for Go development from JetBrains, offering advanced features.[10]

Sublime Text: A powerful text editor with Go plugins.[11]

Configure your chosen IDE or editor with the Go tools and linters you installed to get the best development experience.

6. Hello, World!

Create a file named `main.go` with the following content:

```Go
package main

import "fmt"

func main() {
    fmt.Println("Hello, World! This is Go for DevOps!")
}
```

Navigate to the directory containing `main.go` in your terminal and run:

Bash
go run main.go

You should see "Hello, World! This is Go for DevOps!" printed to the console.

This chapter has equipped you with the fundamental tools and knowledge to start your DevOps journey with Go. In the next chapter, we'll delve into automation.

1.2 Go Fundamentals for Infrastructure Automation

This chapter dives into the essential Go concepts you'll need to effectively automate infrastructure tasks. We'll cover the core language features, standard library packages, and best practices relevant to building robust and maintainable automation scripts. Even if you're already familiar with Go, this chapter will highlight the specific aspects crucial for DevOps and infrastructure automation.

1. Packages and Imports:

Go's package system is fundamental for organizing and reusing code. Every Go program belongs to a package. The `main` package is special; it's the entry point for executable programs. For infrastructure automation, you'll often create your own packages to encapsulate specific functionalities.

Go
package main // This program belongs to the 'main' package

```go
import (
    "fmt" // Importing the 'fmt' package for formatted I/O
        "os"   // Importing the 'os' package for operating system interactions
)

func main() {
    fmt.Println("Hello from the main package!")
        fmt.Println("Current user:", os.Getenv("USER")) // Accessing environment variables
}
```

2. Data Types and Variables:

Go offers a variety of built-in data types, including:

Basic Types: int, float64, string, bool

Composite Types: array, slice, map, struct

Understanding how to declare and manipulate these types is crucial. Slices and maps are particularly important for working with collections of data, which is common in infrastructure automation.

Go
package main

import "fmt"

```go
func main() {
    name := "John Doe" // String variable
    age := 30         // Integer variable
    height := 1.85      // Float variable
    isActive := true    // Boolean variable
```

```go
    servers := []string{"server1", "server2", "server3"} // String slice
    config := map[string]string{
        "environment": "production",
        "region":      "us-east-1",
    } // String map

    fmt.Println("Name:", name)
    fmt.Println("Age:", age)
    fmt.Println("Servers:", servers)
    fmt.Println("Config:", config)

    // Accessing elements:
    fmt.Println("First server:", servers[0])
    fmt.Println("Environment:", config["environment"])
}
```

3. Control Flow:

Control flow statements like `if`, `for`, `switch`, and `select` allow you to control the execution of your code. These are essential for implementing logic and handling different scenarios in your automation scripts.

Go
```go
package main

import "fmt"

func main() {
    for i := 0; i < 5; i++ {
        fmt.Println("Iteration:", i)
    }

    serverStatus := "running"
    switch serverStatus {
```

```go
      case "running":
         fmt.Println("Server is running.")
      case "stopped":
         fmt.Println("Server is stopped.")
      default:
         fmt.Println("Unknown server status.")
   }
}
```

4. Functions:

Functions are the building blocks of Go programs. They allow you to modularize your code and make it more reusable. Understanding how to define and call functions, including passing arguments and returning values, is essential.

Go
```go
package main

import "fmt"

func add(a, b int) int {
   return a + b
}

func greet(name string) {
   fmt.Println("Hello,", name+"!")
}

func main() {
   sum := add(5, 3)
   fmt.Println("Sum:", sum)

   greet("Alice")
}
```

5. Error Handling:

Robust error handling is crucial for infrastructure automation. Go provides mechanisms for returning and handling errors gracefully. Checking errors after function calls is a best practice.

Go
```go
package main

import (
    "fmt"
    "os"
)

func readFile(filename string) (string, error) {
    data, err := os.ReadFile(filename)
    if err != nil {
        return "", fmt.Errorf("error reading file: %w", err) // Wrapping the original error
    }
    return string(data), nil
}

func main() {
    content, err := readFile("myfile.txt")
    if err != nil {
        fmt.Println("Error:", err)
        os.Exit(1) // Exit with an error code
    }
    fmt.Println("File content:", content)
}
```

6. Concurrency with Goroutines and Channels:

Go's built-in concurrency features, goroutines (lightweight threads) and channels (communication channels), are extremely powerful for managing concurrent tasks in infrastructure automation. They allow you to perform operations in parallel, significantly improving performance.

Go

```go
package main

import (
    "fmt"
    "time"
)

func worker(id int, jobs <-chan int, results chan<- int) {
    for j := range jobs {
        fmt.Println("worker", id, "processing job", j)
        time.Sleep(time.Second) // Simulate work
        results <- j * 2
    }
}

func main() {
    const numJobs = 5
    jobs := make(chan int, numJobs)
    results := make(chan int, numJobs)

    // Start worker goroutines
    for w := 1; w <= 3; w++ {
        go worker(w, jobs, results)
    }

    // Send jobs
    for j := 1; j <= numJobs; j++ {
```

```go
        jobs <- j
    }
    close(jobs) // Signal that no more jobs will be sent

    // Receive results
    for a := 1; a <= numJobs; a++ {
        fmt.Println("Result:", <-results)
    }
}
```

These Go fundamentals will provide a strong base for the subsequent chapters, where we'll apply these concepts to automate various infrastructure tasks. Understanding these core principles is crucial for writing efficient, maintainable, and scalable Go-based automation scripts.

1.3 Your First Go DevOps Project

This chapter guides you through creating your first Go DevOps project: a simple yet practical tool to automate checking the status of multiple servers. This project will solidify your understanding of Go fundamentals and introduce you to essential DevOps concepts like interacting with remote systems and handling configuration.

1. Project Setup:

Create a new directory for your project (e.g., server-checker). Navigate into this directory in your terminal and initialize a Go module:

```bash
Bash
mkdir server-checker
cd server-checker
go mod init github.com/yourusername/server-checker  // Replace
with your actual module path
```

Create a file named `main.go` in the project directory. This will be the entry point for your application.

2. Defining Server Configuration:

We'll store the server information (hostname/IP and port) in a configuration file. This makes it easy to manage and modify the servers you want to check without changing the code. Create a file named `config.yaml` in your project directory. We'll use YAML for configuration, but you could also use JSON or other formats.

```yaml
YAML
servers:
  - host: server1.example.com
    port: 80
  - host: 192.168.1.100
    port: 22
  - host: server3.internal
    port: 443
```

3. Reading the Configuration File:

We'll use the `gopkg.in/yaml.v3` package to parse the YAML configuration file. Install it:

```bash
Bash
go get gopkg.in/yaml.v3
```

Now, add the following code to `main.go` to read and parse the configuration:

```go
Go
package main
```

```go
import (
    "fmt"
    "os"
    "gopkg.in/yaml.v3"
    "log"
)

type Server struct {
    Host string `yaml:"host"`
    Port int    `yaml:"port"`
}

type Config struct {
    Servers []Server `yaml:"servers"`
}

func loadConfig(filename string) (*Config, error) {
    data, err := os.ReadFile(filename)
    if err != nil {
        return nil, fmt.Errorf("error reading config file: %w", err)
    }

    var config Config
    err = yaml.Unmarshal(data, &config)
    if err != nil {
        return nil, fmt.Errorf("error unmarshalling config: %w", err)
    }

    return &config, nil
}

func main() {
    config, err := loadConfig("config.yaml")
    if err != nil {
```

```go
        log.Fatal(err)
    }

    fmt.Println("Loaded configuration:")
    for _, server := range config.Servers {
        fmt.Printf("Host: %s, Port: %d\n", server.Host, server.Port)
    }

    // ... (Next step: Checking server status)
}
```

4. Checking Server Status:

We'll use the `net` package to attempt a connection to each server. This is a basic check to see if the server is listening on the specified port.

Go
```go
// ... (Previous code from main.go)

import (
    "fmt"
    "net"
    "os"
    "gopkg.in/yaml.v3"
    "log"
    "time"
)

// ... (Server and Config structs and loadConfig function)


func checkServerStatus(server Server) string {
    target := fmt.Sprintf("%s:%d", server.Host, server.Port)
```

```go
    conn, err := net.DialTimeout("tcp", target, 2*time.Second) //
Timeout after 2 seconds
    if err != nil {
        return fmt.Sprintf("Error: %v", err)
    }
    defer conn.Close() // Close the connection when done

    return "OK"
}

func main() {
    // ... (Load config from previous step)

    fmt.Println("\nChecking server status:")
    for _, server := range config.Servers {
        status := checkServerStatus(server)
        fmt.Printf("%s:%d - %s\n", server.Host, server.Port, status)
    }
}
```

5. Running the Project:

Save the `main.go` file and run the project from your terminal:

Bash
go run main.go

You should see the output showing the loaded configuration and the status of each server.

6. Enhancements (Optional):

More Robust Checks: Instead of just checking the connection, you could implement more sophisticated checks, like sending a specific request and verifying the response.

Concurrency: Use goroutines to check the status of multiple servers concurrently, significantly speeding up the process. You can use a wait group to ensure all checks are completed before the program exits.

Logging: Use a logging library for better output and error handling.

Command-line Arguments: Use the `flag` package to allow users to specify the configuration file or other options via command-line arguments.

Alerting: Integrate with a notification system (e.g., email, Slack) to send alerts when a server is down.

This project provides a basic framework for infrastructure automation. By expanding on these concepts, you can build more complex and powerful tools to manage your infrastructure. This hands-on approach is the best way to learn and apply Go for DevOps.

Chapter 2

Building Command-Line Tools with Go

2.1 Creating Powerful DevOps Utilities with Go

This chapter explores how to build powerful and practical DevOps utilities using Go. We'll delve into advanced techniques, best practices, and real-world examples to help you create tools that streamline your workflows and automate complex tasks.

1. Working with Command-Line Arguments:

The `flag` package allows you to easily parse command-line arguments, making your utilities more flexible and user-friendly.

```go
Go
package main

import (
    "flag"
    "fmt"
)

func main() {
    server := flag.String("server", "localhost", "Server hostname or IP")
    port := flag.Int("port", 8080, "Server port")
    verbose := flag.Bool("v", false, "Enable verbose output")

    flag.Parse() // Parse the command-line arguments

    fmt.Println("Server:", *server)
```

```go
    fmt.Println("Port:", *port)
    fmt.Println("Verbose:", *verbose)

    // ... your utility logic here ...
}
```

To run this: `go run main.go -server my-server.com -port 80 -v`

2. Handling Configuration Files (Advanced):

Beyond simple YAML parsing, consider using libraries like `viper` for more advanced configuration management. `viper` supports multiple configuration formats (YAML, JSON, TOML), environment variables, and remote configuration sources.

```go
Go
package main

import (
    "fmt"
    "log"

    "github.com/spf13/viper"
)

func main() {
    viper.SetConfigName("config") // Name of config file (without extension)
    viper.SetConfigType("yaml")   // Type of config file (yaml, json, toml)
    viper.AddConfigPath(".")      // Search current directory for config file
    viper.AddConfigPath("/etc/myapp/") // Search /etc/myapp/ for config file
```

```go
        viper.AddConfigPath("$HOME/.myapp")    //    Search
$HOME/.myapp for config file

    if err := viper.ReadInConfig(); err != nil {
        if _, ok := err.(viper.ConfigFileNotFoundError); ok {
            // Config file not found; ignore if desired
            fmt.Println("No config file found, using defaults")
        } else {
            log.Fatal(fmt.Errorf("fatal error config file: %w", err))
        }
    }

    server := viper.GetString("server")
    port := viper.GetInt("port")

    fmt.Println("Server:", server)
    fmt.Println("Port:", port)
}
```

3. Logging and Error Handling (Best Practices):

Effective logging is essential for debugging and monitoring your utilities. Use a structured logging library like logrus or zap for more informative logs.

Go
```go
package main

import (
    "os"

    log "github.com/sirupsen/logrus"
)

func main() {
```

```go
log.SetFormatter(&log.JSONFormatter{}) // Use JSON formatter
log.SetOutput(os.Stdout)               // Output to stdout

log.WithFields(log.Fields{
   "animal": "walrus",
}).Info("A walrus appears")

log.WithFields(log.Fields{
   "animal": "seal",
   "size":   "large",
}).Warn("A large seal appears")

// For errors:
err := someFunctionThatMightFail()
if err != nil {
   log.WithError(err).Error("Something failed")
}
}
```

4. Interacting with External Systems (SSH, HTTP, Cloud APIs):

Go's standard library and third-party packages provide tools for interacting with various systems:

SSH: The `crypto/ssh` package allows you to execute commands on remote servers.

HTTP: The `net/http` package is used for making HTTP requests and building web servers. Consider using a more feature-rich HTTP client library like `fasthttp` or `resty`.

Cloud APIs: Cloud providers (AWS, GCP, Azure) offer Go SDKs for interacting with their services.

Example (SSH):

```go
Go
package main

import (
    "fmt"
    "log"
    "golang.org/x/crypto/ssh"
)

func main() {
    config := &ssh.ClientConfig{
        User: "youruser",
        Auth: &ssh.Password("yourpassword"), // In real-world, use key-based auth
        HostKeyCallback: ssh.InsecureIgnoreHostKey(), // Insecure for demo, use proper host key verification
    }
    client, err := ssh.Dial("tcp", "yourserver:22", config)
    if err != nil {
        log.Fatal("dial failed:", err)
    }
    defer client.Close()

    session, err := client.NewSession()
    if err != nil {
        log.Fatal("session failed:", err)
    }
    defer session.Close()

    cmd := "ls -l" // Command to execute
    out, err := session.CombinedOutput([]byte(cmd))
    if err != nil {
        log.Fatal("command failed:", err)
```

```
    }
    fmt.Printf("%s\n", out)
}
```

5. Building and Distributing Your Utilities:

Use `go build` to compile your utilities into standalone executables. Consider using tools like `goreleaser` to automate the release process, including creating binaries for different platforms, generating checksums, and publishing releases to GitHub or other platforms.

6. Testing:

Write unit and integration tests to ensure the reliability of your utilities. The `testing` package in Go provides the necessary tools for testing.

7. Example: A Simple HTTP Server Monitoring Utility:

Go

```
// ... (Imports, config, logging setup)

func checkHTTPStatus(url string) (int, error) {
    resp, err := http.Get(url)
    if err != nil {
        return 0, err
    }
    defer resp.Body.Close()
    return resp.StatusCode, nil
}

func main() {
    // ... (Load config)
```

```go
    for _, server := range config.Servers {
        url := fmt.Sprintf("http://%s:%d", server.Host, server.Port)
        status, err := checkHTTPStatus(url)
        if err != nil {
            log.WithError(err).Errorf("Error checking %s", url)
        } else {
            log.Infof("%s: Status %d", url, status)
        }
    }
}
```

This enhanced example demonstrates how to combine configuration, error handling, logging, and external system interaction to create a useful DevOps utility. Remember to install the necessary packages (e.g., `logrus`, `viper`) using `go get`. This chapter provided a foundation for creating powerful DevOps utilities. By combining these techniques and exploring relevant Go packages, you can build tools that significantly improve your DevOps workflows.

2.2 Go's Standard Library for DevOps Tasks

Go's standard library is a treasure trove of tools for DevOps tasks. It provides built-in packages that cover a wide range of functionalities, from basic I/O and networking to more advanced features like cryptography and compression. Leveraging the standard library can simplify your DevOps scripting and reduce external dependencies.

1. File and Directory Operations (`os`, `io`, `path/filepath`):

These packages provide functions for working with files and directories:

`os`: Provides functions for interacting with the operating system, including file creation, deletion, renaming, and working with environment variables.

`io`: Provides interfaces and functions for I/O operations, such as reading and writing files, working with buffers, and handling streams.

`path/filepath`: Provides functions for manipulating file paths, including joining paths, extracting file extensions, and walking directory trees.

Go

```go
package main

import (
    "fmt"
    "io/ioutil"
    "os"
    "path/filepath"
)

func main() {
    // Create a directory
    err := os.Mkdir("mydir", 0755) // Permissions: read/write/execute
for owner, read and execute for group and others
    if err != nil {
        fmt.Println("Error creating directory:", err)
    }

    // Create a file
    file, err := os.Create("mydir/myfile.txt")
    if err != nil {
        fmt.Println("Error creating file:", err)
    }
    defer file.Close() // Always close files
```

```go
    // Write to the file
    _, err = file.WriteString("Hello, DevOps with Go!\n")
    if err != nil {
        fmt.Println("Error writing to file:", err)
    }

    // Read the file content
    data, err := ioutil.ReadFile("mydir/myfile.txt")
    if err != nil {
        fmt.Println("Error reading file:", err)
    }
    fmt.Println("File content:", string(data))

    // Walk a directory tree
    err = filepath.Walk(".", func(path string, info os.FileInfo, err error) error {
        if err != nil {
            return err
        }
        fmt.Println("Visited:", path)
        return nil
    })
    if err != nil {
        fmt.Println("Error walking directory:", err)
    }

    // Remove a file
    err = os.Remove("mydir/myfile.txt")
    if err != nil {
        fmt.Println("Error removing file:", err)
    }

    // Remove a directory
```

```go
    err = os.RemoveAll("mydir") // Removes directory and its
contents
    if err != nil {
        fmt.Println("Error removing directory:", err)
    }
}
```

2. Networking (net):

The net package provides functionalities for network programming, including working with TCP and UDP connections, resolving hostnames, and building network servers. We used this in the server status check example earlier.

Go
```go
package main

import (
    "fmt"
    "net"
)

func main() {
    // Resolve a hostname
    addrs, err := net.LookupHost("google.com")
    if err != nil {
        fmt.Println("Error resolving hostname:", err)
    }
    fmt.Println("Addresses for google.com:", addrs)

    // Dial a TCP connection
    conn, err := net.Dial("tcp", "google.com:80")
    if err != nil {
        fmt.Println("Error dialing connection:", err)
    }
```

```go
    defer conn.Close()

    fmt.Println("Connected to google.com:80")
}
```

3. HTTP Client and Server (net/http):

The net/http package provides tools for making HTTP requests and building HTTP servers.

Go
```go
package main

import (
    "fmt"
    "net/http"
    "io/ioutil"
)

func main() {
    // Make an HTTP GET request
    resp, err := http.Get("https://example.com")
    if err != nil {
        fmt.Println("Error making request:", err)
    }
    defer resp.Body.Close()

    // Read the response body
    body, err := ioutil.ReadAll(resp.Body)
    if err != nil {
        fmt.Println("Error reading response:", err)
    }
    fmt.Println("Response:", string(body))
```

```go
    // Start a simple HTTP server
        http.HandleFunc("/", func(w http.ResponseWriter, r *http.Request) {
        fmt.Fprintf(w, "Hello, World from Go HTTP Server!")
    })

    fmt.Println("Server listening on port 8080")
    http.ListenAndServe(":8080", nil)

}
```

4. JSON and Encoding (`encoding/json`):

The `encoding/json` package provides functions for encoding and decoding JSON data, which is commonly used in APIs and data exchange.

Go
```go
package main

import (
    "encoding/json"
    "fmt"
)

type Person struct {
    Name  string `json:"name"`
    Age   int    `json:"age"`
    Email string `json:"email,omitempty"` // omitempty: field is omitted if empty
}

func main() {
    person := Person{Name: "John Doe", Age: 30}
```

```go
    // Marshal (encode) to JSON
    jsonData, err := json.MarshalIndent(person, "", "   ") // Use
MarshalIndent for pretty printing
    if err != nil {
        fmt.Println("Error marshalling JSON:", err)
    }
    fmt.Println(string(jsonData))

    // Unmarshal (decode) from JSON
    var anotherPerson Person
    err = json.Unmarshal(jsonData, &anotherPerson)
    if err != nil {
        fmt.Println("Error unmarshalling JSON:", err)
    }
    fmt.Println("Unmarshalled person:", anotherPerson)
}
```

5. Time and Date (`time`):

The `time` package provides functions for working with dates and times.

Go
```go
package main

import (
    "fmt"
    "time"
)

func main() {
    now := time.Now()
    fmt.Println("Current time:", now)
```

```
        fmt.Println("Formatted   time:",   now.Format("2006-01-02
15:04:05")) // Example format

    futureTime := now.Add(24 * time.Hour) // Add 24 hours
    fmt.Println("Future time:", futureTime)

    elapsed := time.Since(now)
    fmt.Println("Time elapsed:", elapsed)
}
```

6. Compression (`compress/gzip`, `compress/flate`):

The `compress` packages offer support for various compression formats, which can be useful for reducing the size of data transferred over the network or stored on disk.

7. Template Processing (`text/template`):

The `text/template` package allows you to generate text output based on templates, which can be useful for configuration file generation or report generation.

8. Hashing and Cryptography (`crypto`):

The `crypto` package provides tools for cryptographic operations, including hashing, encryption, and digital signatures.

These are just a few examples of the many useful packages in Go's standard library. By exploring the documentation and experimenting with these packages, you can significantly enhance your DevOps scripting capabilities and build powerful tools without relying heavily on external dependencies. Remember to refer to the official Go documentation for the most up-to-date information and details on each package.

2.3 CLI Design and Best Practices in Go

Command-line interfaces (CLIs) are essential tools in the DevOps world. A well-designed CLI makes your Go utilities easy to use, understand, and integrate into automation workflows. This chapter covers best practices for designing and implementing effective CLIs in Go.

1. Choosing a CLI Library:

While you *can* use the `flag` package for simple CLIs, dedicated libraries offer more features and a better user experience. Popular choices include:

Cobra: A powerful and widely used library for creating complex CLIs with nested commands, flags, and help generation. It's used by projects like Kubernetes and Hugo.

CLI: A simpler and more lightweight library compared to Cobra, suitable for less complex CLIs.

urfave/cli (formerly codegangsta/cli): Another popular option known for its ease of use.

We'll focus on Cobra in this chapter due to its popularity and feature set.

2. Structuring Your CLI with Cobra:

Cobra encourages a structured approach, making your CLI code more organized and maintainable. A typical Cobra CLI consists of:

Root Command: The main command of your CLI (e.g., `myapp`).

Subcommands: Commands nested under the root command (e.g., `myapp server start`, `myapp database migrate`).

Flags: Options that modify the behavior of commands (e.g., `--config`, `--verbose`).

Go
```go
package main

import (
    "fmt"
    "os"

    "github.com/spf13/cobra"
)

var configFile string
var verbose bool

var rootCmd = &cobra.Command{
    Use:   "myapp",
    Short: "A brief description of your application",
    Long: `A longer description that spans multiple lines.
This is the extended description.`,
    Run: func(cmd *cobra.Command, args []string) {
        fmt.Println("This is the root command.")
            if verbose {
                    fmt.Println("Verbose mode enabled")
            }
            fmt.Println("Config file: ", configFile)
    },
}

var serverCmd = &cobra.Command{
    Use:   "server",
    Short: "Manage servers",
}
```

```go
var serverStartCmd = &cobra.Command{
    Use:   "start",
    Short: "Start a server",
    Run: func(cmd *cobra.Command, args []string) {
        fmt.Println("Starting server...")
        // ... server start logic ...
    },
}

func init() {
    rootCmd.PersistentFlags().StringVarP(&configFile, "config", "c",
"config.yaml", "Configuration file")
    rootCmd.PersistentFlags().BoolVarP(&verbose, "verbose", "v",
false, "Enable verbose output")
    serverCmd.AddCommand(serverStartCmd)
    rootCmd.AddCommand(serverCmd)
}

func main() {
    if err := rootCmd.Execute(); err != nil {
        fmt.Println(err)
        os.Exit(1)
    }
}
```

3. Defining Flags:

Cobra supports different types of flags:

Persistent Flags: Available to the root command and all its subcommands.

Local Flags: Only available to a specific command.

Use the `PersistentFlags()` and `Flags()` methods to define flags.

4. Handling Arguments:

Commands can also accept arguments. You can access these arguments using the `args` parameter in the command's `Run` function.

```go
Go
var serverStartCmd = &cobra.Command{
    Use:    "start [server-name]", // [server-name] indicates an argument
    Short: "Start a server",
    Args:  cobra.ExactArgs(1), // Ensure exactly 1 argument is provided
    Run: func(cmd *cobra.Command, args []string) {
        serverName := args[0]
        fmt.Printf("Starting server: %s\n", serverName)
        // ... server start logic ...
    },
}
```

5. Generating Help and Documentation:

Cobra automatically generates help messages based on your command and flag descriptions. You can customize the help output if needed.

6. Input Validation:

Validate user input (flags and arguments) to prevent errors and ensure your CLI behaves correctly. Cobra provides functions like `cobra.ExactArgs` and `cobra.MinimumNArgs` for basic argument validation. You can also implement custom validation logic.

7. Error Handling:

Handle errors gracefully and provide informative error messages to the user. Use Go's error handling mechanisms and consider using a logging library for more detailed error reporting.

8. Testing:

Write unit and integration tests for your CLI to ensure its reliability and correctness. Test different combinations of commands, flags, and arguments.

9. Example: A Simple Backup Utility:

```go
Go
// ... (imports, rootCmd setup)

var backupCmd = &cobra.Command{
    Use:   "backup <source> <destination>",
    Short: "Backup files",
    Args: cobra.ExactArgs(2),
    Run: func(cmd *cobra.Command, args []string) {
        source := args[0]
        destination := args[1]

        fmt.Printf("Backing up %s to %s\n", source, destination)
        // ... backup logic (using os, io, etc.) ...
    },
}

func init() {
    rootCmd.AddCommand(backupCmd)
}
```

```
// ... (main function)
```

This example demonstrates how to use Cobra to create a simple backup utility with source and destination arguments.

By following these best practices, you can create well-designed, user-friendly, and maintainable CLIs in Go that are essential for effective DevOps automation. Remember to consult the Cobra documentation for more advanced features and customization options.

Chapter 3

Working with APIs in Go

3.1 Integrating with Cloud Providers and Services

Modern DevOps heavily relies on cloud providers and their services. This chapter explores how to integrate your Go applications and utilities with popular cloud platforms like AWS, Google Cloud Platform (GCP), and Azure, as well as other cloud-native services.

1. Authentication and Authorization:

Before interacting with any cloud service, you need to authenticate your application and grant it the necessary permissions. Each cloud provider has its own authentication mechanisms:

AWS: Typically uses Access Keys (Access Key ID and Secret Access Key) or IAM roles for EC2 instances. AWS also supports more advanced authentication methods like AWS SSO.

GCP: Uses service accounts, which are special Google accounts that represent your application. You'll need to download a service account key file.

Azure: Uses service principals, similar to service accounts in GCP. You'll need a client ID, client secret, and tenant ID.

2. Using Cloud SDKs:

Cloud providers offer Go SDKs that simplify the process of interacting with their services. These SDKs provide pre-built functions and data structures for common operations, handling authentication, request formatting, and response parsing.

AWS SDK for Go: `github.com/aws/aws-sdk-go/aws`

Google Cloud Go Client Libraries: `cloud.google.com/go`

Azure SDK for Go: `github.com/Azure/azure-sdk-for-go`

3. Example: Listing S3 Buckets (AWS):

```go
Go
package main

import (
    "fmt"
    "log"

    "github.com/aws/aws-sdk-go/aws"
    "github.com/aws/aws-sdk-go/aws/session"
    "github.com/aws/aws-sdk-go/service/s3"
)

func main() {
    // Load AWS credentials from environment variables, shared credentials file, or EC2 instance metadata.
    sess, err := session.Must(session.NewSessionWithOptions(session.Options{
        SharedConfigState: session.SharedConfigEnable, // Load shared config
    }))

    svc := s3.New(sess)

    result, err := svc.ListBuckets(nil)
    if err != nil {
```

```go
        log.Fatal("Unable to list buckets:", err)
    }

    fmt.Println("Buckets:")
    for _, b := range result.Buckets {
        fmt.Printf("* %s\n", aws.StringValue(b.Name))
    }
}
```

4. Example: Listing Compute Instances (GCP):

```go
Go
package main

import (
        "context"
        "fmt"
        "log"

        "google.golang.org/api/compute/v1"
        "google.golang.org/api/option"
)

func main() {
        // Replace with your project ID
        projectID := "your-project-id"

        // Authenticate using a service account key file
        ctx := context.Background()
                computeService, err := compute.NewService(ctx,
option.WithCredentialsFile("path/to/your/service_account_key.json
"))
        if err != nil {
                log.Fatal(err)
```

```go
    }

    // List instances in a zone
    zone := "your-zone"
     instanceList, err := computeService.Instances.List(projectID,
zone).Do()
    if err != nil {
        log.Fatal(err)
    }

    fmt.Println("Instances in", zone+":")
    for _, instance := range instanceList.Items {
        fmt.Println("-", instance.Name)
    }
}
```

5. Example: Listing Virtual Machines (Azure):

```go
Go
package main

import (
    "context"
    "fmt"
    "log"

    "github.com/Azure/azure-sdk-for-go/sdk/azcore/identity"

"github.com/Azure/azure-sdk-for-go/sdk/resourcemanager/comput
e/armcompute/v5" // Use appropriate version
)

func main() {
    // Replace with your subscription ID, resource group, and
location
```

```go
    subscriptionID := "your-subscription-id"
    resourceGroupName := "your-resource-group"
    location := "your-location"

    // Authenticate using managed identity or service principal
    cred, err := identity.NewDefaultAzureCredential(nil)
    if err != nil {
        log.Fatal(err)
    }

    // Create a compute client
    computeClient, err := armcompute.NewVirtualMachinesClient(subscriptionID, cred, nil)
    if err != nil {
        log.Fatal(err)
    }

    // List VMs
    pager := computeClient.List(resourceGroupName, nil)
    for pager.NextPage(context.TODO()) {
        resp, err := pager.PageResponse()
        if err != nil {
            log.Fatal(err)
        }
        for _, vm := range resp.Value {
            fmt.Println("-", *vm.Name)
        }
    }

    if err := pager.Err(); err != nil {
        log.Fatal(err)
    }
}
```

6. Working with Cloud-Native Services:

Beyond core compute services, cloud providers offer a wide range of managed services (databases, message queues, serverless functions, etc.). The respective SDKs provide access to these services as well.

7. Environment Variables and Configuration:

Store cloud credentials and other sensitive information in environment variables or use a dedicated configuration management system. Avoid hardcoding credentials directly in your code.

8. Error Handling and Retries:

Cloud service interactions can be prone to transient errors. Implement proper error handling and retry mechanisms to make your applications more resilient.

9. Testing:

Test your cloud integrations thoroughly. Consider using mocks or emulators for unit testing and integration tests against actual cloud environments (with appropriate precautions).

10. Best Practices:

Follow the principle of least privilege. Grant your applications only the necessary permissions.

Use secure authentication methods (e.g., IAM roles, managed identities).

Handle rate limiting and throttling appropriately.

Monitor your cloud resources and costs.

This chapter provided a basic overview of integrating with cloud providers and services. Consult the documentation for the specific cloud provider and service you are using for more detailed information and examples. Remember to install the necessary SDKs using `go get`. By mastering cloud integrations, you can build powerful and scalable DevOps solutions.

3.2 RESTful API Consumption and Creation in Go

RESTful API Consumption and Creation in Go

RESTful APIs are the backbone of modern web applications and microservices. This chapter explores how to both consume (interact with) and create (build) RESTful APIs using Go.

Part 1: Consuming RESTful APIs

1. Making HTTP Requests:

Go's `net/http` package is the foundation for making HTTP requests. For simpler use cases, it's often sufficient. For more complex scenarios, consider using `fasthttp` or `resty` for better performance and features.

Go
```
package main

import (
    "encoding/json"
    "fmt"
    "log"
    "net/http"
    "io/ioutil"
)
```

```go
type User struct {
    ID    int    `json:"id"`
    Name  string `json:"name"`
    Email string `json:"email"`
}

func main() {
    // Make a GET request
    resp, err := http.Get("https://jsonplaceholder.typicode.com/users/1") // Example API endpoint
    if err != nil {
        log.Fatal(err)
    }
    defer resp.Body.Close()

    // Read the response body
    body, err := ioutil.ReadAll(resp.Body)
    if err != nil {
        log.Fatal(err)
    }

    // Unmarshal the JSON response into a struct
    var user User
    err = json.Unmarshal(body, &user)
    if err != nil {
        log.Fatal(err)
    }

    fmt.Println("User:", user)


    //Example POST request
```

```go
        newUser := User{Name: "Jane Doe", Email:
"jane.doe@example.com"}
    jsonValue, _ := json.Marshal(newUser)

                                        resp,      err      =
http.Post("https://jsonplaceholder.typicode.com/users",
"application/json",  ioutil.NopCloser(bytes.NewBuffer(jsonValue)))

    if err != nil {
        log.Fatal(err)
    }

    defer resp.Body.Close()

    body, err = ioutil.ReadAll(resp.Body)

    if err != nil {
        log.Fatal(err)
    }

    fmt.Println(string(body))


}
```

2. Handling Different HTTP Methods:

RESTful APIs use different HTTP methods for different actions:

GET: Retrieve data

POST: Create new data

PUT: Update existing data

DELETE: Delete data

Use `http.Post`, `http.NewRequest` (for custom methods like PUT and DELETE), or libraries like `resty` to make requests with different methods.

3. Setting Headers:

You can set headers in your HTTP requests using the `req.Header` property (where `req` is an `*http.Request`). This is often necessary for authentication, specifying content types, etc.

4. Handling Responses:

Check the HTTP status code of the response to determine if the request was successful. A 2xx status code generally indicates success. Handle errors appropriately based on the status code.

5. Authentication:

Many APIs require authentication. Common methods include:

API Keys: Often passed in headers or query parameters.

OAuth: A more complex authorization framework.

Basic Authentication: Username and password.

6. Using `resty` (for more advanced use cases):

```
Go
package main

import (
    "fmt"
    "log"
```

```go
    "github.com/go-resty/resty/v2"
)

type User struct {
    ID    int    `json:"id"`
    Name  string `json:"name"`
    Email string `json:"email"`
}

func main() {
    client := resty.New()

    // GET request
    user := User{} // Create an empty struct to unmarshal into
    _, err := client.R().
        SetResult(&user). // Set the struct to unmarshal into
        Get("https://jsonplaceholder.typicode.com/users/1")

    if err != nil {
        log.Fatal(err)
    }

    fmt.Println("User:", user)


    //POST request
            newUser := User{Name: "Jane Doe", Email:
"jane.doe@example.com"}

    resp, err := client.R().
        SetBody(newUser).
        Post("https://jsonplaceholder.typicode.com/users")

    if err != nil {
```

```go
        log.Fatal(err)
    }

    fmt.Println(resp)

}
```

Part 2: Creating RESTful APIs

1. Setting up an HTTP Server:

Use the net/http package to create an HTTP server in Go.

Go

```go
package main

import (
    "encoding/json"
    "fmt"
    "log"
    "net/http"
)

type User struct {
    ID    int    `json:"id"`
    Name  string `json:"name"`
    Email string `json:"email"`
}

var users = []User{
    {ID: 1, Name: "John Doe", Email: "john.doe@example.com"},
    {ID: 2, Name: "Jane Doe", Email: "jane.doe@example.com"},
}
```

```go
func getUsers(w http.ResponseWriter, r *http.Request) {
    w.Header().Set("Content-Type", "application/json")
    json.NewEncoder(w).Encode(users)
}

func main() {
    http.HandleFunc("/users", getUsers) // Define API endpoints

    fmt.Println("Server listening on port 8080")
    log.Fatal(http.ListenAndServe(":8080", nil))
}
```

2. Handling Routes:

Use `http.HandleFunc` to register handlers for different URL paths. For more complex routing, consider using a router library like `gorilla/mux`.

3. Handling HTTP Methods:

Implement different handler functions for different HTTP methods (GET, POST, PUT, DELETE) to handle different API actions.

4. Request and Response Handling:

Request: Access request data (query parameters, request body) using the `r *http.Request` object.

Response: Write responses using the `w http.ResponseWriter` object. Set headers, status codes, and write the response body (often JSON).

5. Data Serialization and Deserialization:

Use the `encoding/json` package to marshal (encode) Go structs into JSON for responses and unmarshal (decode) JSON from requests into Go structs.

6. Error Handling:

Implement proper error handling to return appropriate HTTP status codes and error messages to the client.

7. Middleware:

Middleware functions can be used to add common functionality to your API endpoints, such as authentication, logging, or request validation.

8. API Documentation:

Document your API using tools like Swagger or OpenAPI to make it easier for clients to use.

This chapter provided a foundation for both consuming and creating RESTful APIs in Go. Remember to explore the Go documentation and the documentation for any third-party libraries you are using for more in-depth information and examples. Building and consuming RESTful APIs is a core skill for any DevOps engineer working with modern distributed systems.

3.3 Building API-Driven Automation with Go

This chapter focuses on building API-driven automation using Go. We'll explore how to combine the API consumption and creation techniques from the previous chapter with other DevOps skills to create powerful automated workflows. This approach allows you to orchestrate complex tasks by interacting with various services and systems through their APIs.

1. Designing Your Automation Workflow:

Before diving into code, carefully design your automation workflow. Consider the following:

What tasks need to be automated? (e.g., server provisioning, application deployments, monitoring, scaling)

What APIs will you interact with? (e.g., cloud provider APIs, CI/CD system APIs, monitoring tool APIs)

What are the dependencies between tasks? (e.g., deploy application only after server is provisioned)

What are the error handling and retry strategies?

How will you trigger the automation? (e.g., on a schedule, in response to an event, manually)

2. Implementing API Interactions:

Use the techniques from the previous chapter to interact with the necessary APIs. This includes making HTTP requests, handling responses, and authenticating with the APIs.

3. Orchestrating Tasks:

Use Go's concurrency features (goroutines and channels) to orchestrate multiple API calls and tasks. This allows you to perform operations in parallel and manage dependencies between them.

```go
Go
package main

import (
    "context"
    "fmt"
```

```go
	"log"
	"time"

	// ... other imports
)

func provisionServer(ctx context.Context, serverName string) error {
	// ... API call to provision server (e.g., using cloud provider SDK)
...
	fmt.Println("Provisioning server:", serverName)
	time.Sleep(2 * time.Second) // Simulate provisioning time
	return nil // Or return an error if provisioning fails
}

func deployApplication(ctx context.Context, serverName string) error {
	// ... API call to deploy application (e.g., using CI/CD API) ...
	fmt.Println("Deploying application to:", serverName)
	time.Sleep(2 * time.Second) // Simulate deployment time
	return nil // Or return an error if deployment fails
}

func monitorServer(ctx context.Context, serverName string) error {
	// ... API call to monitor server (e.g., using monitoring tool API)
...
	fmt.Println("Monitoring server:", serverName)
	time.Sleep(2 * time.Second) // Simulate monitoring
	return nil // Or return an error if monitoring fails
}

func main() {
	ctx := context.Background() // Or use a context with timeout or
cancellation
```

```go
    servers := []string{"server1", "server2", "server3"}

    for _, server := range servers {
        go func(serverName string) {
            err := provisionServer(ctx, serverName)
            if err != nil {
                log.Printf("Error provisioning %s: %v", serverName, err)
                return
            }

            err = deployApplication(ctx, serverName)
            if err != nil {
                log.Printf("Error deploying to %s: %v", serverName, err)
                return
            }

            err = monitorServer(ctx, serverName)
            if err != nil {
                log.Printf("Error monitoring %s: %v", serverName, err)
                return
            }

                    fmt.Println(serverName + " finished")
        }(server)
    }

        time.Sleep(10 * time.Second) // Wait for goroutines to finish
(or use a WaitGroup)

    fmt.Println("Automation complete.")
}
```

4. Handling Errors and Retries:

Implement robust error handling and retry mechanisms to make your automation more resilient. Use Go's error handling features and consider using a retry library.

5. Configuration Management:

Store API keys, credentials, and other configuration data securely. Use environment variables, configuration files, or dedicated configuration management tools like HashiCorp Vault.

6. Logging and Monitoring:

Use a logging library (e.g., `logrus`, `zap`) to log important events and errors during the automation process. Integrate with a monitoring system to track the progress and health of your automation.

7. Triggering Automation:

Scheduled Tasks: Use cron jobs or task schedulers to run your automation on a schedule.

Event-Driven: Trigger your automation in response to events (e.g., a new code commit, a cloud resource change). This often involves webhooks or message queues.

Manual Triggers: Create a simple CLI or web interface to trigger your automation manually.

8. Example: Automated Application Deployment:

This example shows a simplified workflow for automatically deploying an application to a server after a code commit.

Code Commit: A developer commits code to a Git repository (e.g., GitHub, GitLab).

Webhook Trigger: The Git platform sends a webhook to your Go application.

API Call to CI/CD: Your Go application receives the webhook and makes an API call to your CI/CD system (e.g., Jenkins, GitLab CI) to trigger a build.

Build and Deployment: The CI/CD system builds the application and deploys it to the server via API calls (e.g., SSH, cloud provider APIs).

Notification: Your Go application receives a notification from the CI/CD system that the deployment is complete. It might then send a notification to a Slack channel or update a monitoring dashboard.

9. Best Practices:

Idempotency: Design your automation to be idempotent, meaning it can be run multiple times without causing unintended side effects.

Testing: Thoroughly test your automation scripts to ensure they work as expected.

Security: Securely manage API keys and credentials.

Documentation: Document your automation workflows and code.

By combining API interaction skills with Go's concurrency and other features, you can build powerful and flexible API-driven automation solutions for a wide range of DevOps tasks. Remember to carefully design your workflows, handle errors effectively, and prioritize security.

Chapter 4

Infrastructure as Code with Go

4.1 Managing Infrastructure with Go and Terraform

Terraform has become a standard tool for Infrastructure as Code (IaC), allowing you to define and manage your infrastructure in a declarative way. Go can be effectively combined with Terraform to create powerful and flexible infrastructure management solutions. This chapter explores how to use Go alongside Terraform to automate and enhance your infrastructure management workflows.

1. Understanding the Synergy:

Terraform: Handles the provisioning and management of infrastructure resources (servers, networks, databases, etc.) using configuration files written in HashiCorp Configuration Language (HCL) or JSON.

Go: Provides a general-purpose programming language for building tools and applications that interact with Terraform. This allows you to create custom logic, handle complex workflows, and integrate with other systems.

2. Interacting with Terraform Programmatically:

Go can interact with Terraform in several ways:

Terraform CLI: You can execute Terraform commands (e.g., `plan`, `apply`, `destroy`) from your Go code using the `os/exec` package. This is a straightforward approach for simple use cases.

Terraform Plugin SDK: For more advanced scenarios, you can use the Terraform Plugin SDK to develop custom Terraform providers or extend existing ones. This allows you to manage resources that are not directly supported by existing providers.

Go bindings for the Terraform Core: These provide lower-level access to Terraform's internals, enabling more fine-grained control. This approach is typically used for building tools that deeply integrate with Terraform.

3. Simple Example: Running Terraform Commands from Go:

Go
```go
package main

import (
    "fmt"
    "log"
    "os/exec"
)

func main() {
    // Define the Terraform working directory
    terraformDir := "./terraform" // Replace with your Terraform directory

    // Execute 'terraform init'
    cmd := exec.Command("terraform", "init")
    cmd.Dir = terraformDir // Set the working directory
    output, err := cmd.CombinedOutput() // Capture both stdout and stderr
    if err != nil {
        log.Fatalf("terraform init failed: %v\n%s", err, output)
    }
    fmt.Println(string(output))
```

```go
    // Execute 'terraform apply'
    cmd = exec.Command("terraform", "apply", "-auto-approve") // -auto-approve for non-interactive use
    cmd.Dir = terraformDir
    output, err = cmd.CombinedOutput()
    if err != nil {
        log.Fatalf("terraform apply failed: %v\n%s", err, output)
    }
    fmt.Println(string(output))

    fmt.Println("Terraform apply complete.")
}
```

4. Advanced Use Cases:

Dynamic Infrastructure Generation: Use Go to generate Terraform configuration files dynamically based on various inputs (e.g., configuration files, databases, APIs). This is useful for creating reusable infrastructure modules and managing complex deployments.

Custom Provisioning Logic: Implement custom provisioning logic in Go that interacts with Terraform. For example, you might need to perform certain actions before or after Terraform provisions resources.

Integration with CI/CD: Integrate Terraform with your CI/CD pipeline using Go. This allows you to automate infrastructure deployments as part of your software delivery process.

Infrastructure Testing: Use Go to write automated tests for your infrastructure. You can use tools like Terratest to verify that your infrastructure is configured correctly.

Terraform Cloud or Enterprise APIs: Go can be used to interact with the Terraform Cloud or Enterprise APIs for managing workspaces, running plans, and applying changes remotely.

5. Example: Dynamic Terraform Configuration Generation:

```go
Go
package main

import (
    "fmt"
    "log"
    "os"
    "text/template"
)

type Server struct {
    Name    string
    Size    string
    Region  string
}

func main() {
    servers := []Server{
            {Name: "web-server-1", Size: "t2.medium", Region: "us-east-1"},
            {Name: "db-server-1", Size: "db.t3.micro", Region: "us-west-2"},
    }

    // Create a Terraform template
    tmpl, err := template.New("terraform.tf").Parse(`
resource "aws_instance" "{{ .Name }}" {
  ami           = "ami-0c94855ba95c574c8" # Replace with your AMI
  instance_type = "{{ .Size }}"
  region = "{{ .Region }}"
```

```go
  tags = {
    Name = "{{ .Name }}"
   }
}
`)

    if err != nil {
       log.Fatal(err)
    }

    // Generate Terraform configuration for each server
    for _, server := range servers {
           filename := fmt.Sprintf("./terraform/%s.tf", server.Name) //
Create separate files
        f, err := os.Create(filename)
        if err != nil {
           log.Fatal(err)
        }
        err = tmpl.Execute(f, server)
        if err != nil {
           log.Fatal(err)
        }
        f.Close()
           fmt.Printf("Generated Terraform configuration for %s\n",
server.Name)
     }

    fmt.Println("Terraform configuration generation complete.")

       // ... (Then run 'terraform init' and 'terraform apply' as in the
previous example)
}
```

6. Best Practices:

Version Control: Keep your Terraform code and Go scripts in version control.

Modularization: Break down your infrastructure into smaller, reusable modules.

Testing: Test your infrastructure code thoroughly.

Security: Securely manage Terraform state files and any credentials used by your Go scripts.

Automation: Automate your infrastructure deployments using CI/CD pipelines.

By combining the power of Terraform with the flexibility of Go, you can create robust and efficient infrastructure management solutions. Go allows you to extend Terraform's capabilities and tailor it to your specific needs. Remember to install the required Go packages (if any) using `go get`.

4.2 Automating Cloud Deployments with Go

This chapter delves into automating cloud deployments using Go. We'll explore various techniques and best practices for building robust and efficient deployment pipelines that leverage Go's capabilities.

1. Understanding the Deployment Process:

Before automating, it's crucial to understand the steps involved in your deployment process. This typically includes:

Building the application: Compiling your Go code and creating any necessary artifacts (e.g., binaries, Docker images).

Packaging: Creating deployable packages (e.g., Docker images, zip files).

Infrastructure provisioning: Setting up the necessary infrastructure (servers, databases, load balancers). This can be done with Terraform or other IaC tools (as covered in the previous chapter).

Deployment: Copying or deploying the application package to the target infrastructure.

Testing: Running automated tests to verify the deployment.

Rollback: Having a strategy for rolling back to a previous version if the deployment fails.

2. Choosing Deployment Strategies:

Different deployment strategies cater to different needs:

Blue/Green Deployments: Run two identical environments (blue and green). Deploy the new version to the inactive environment (e.g., green), test it, and then switch traffic from blue to green.

Canary Deployments: Deploy the new version to a small subset of users or servers (the "canary"). If everything goes well, gradually roll out the deployment to the rest of the infrastructure.

Rolling Updates: Update servers or instances one at a time or in batches. This minimizes downtime but requires careful orchestration.

3. Building Deployment Tools with Go:

Go is well-suited for building deployment tools due to its concurrency features, standard library, and strong support for networking and interacting with cloud APIs.

4. Example: Building a Simple Deployment Tool:

This example demonstrates a basic deployment tool that copies a binary to a remote server via SSH.

Go
```go
package main

import (
    "fmt"
    "log"
    "os/exec"

    "golang.org/x/crypto/ssh"
)

func deploy(server, user, binaryPath string) error {
    config := &ssh.ClientConfig{
        User: user,
        Auth: &ssh.Password("yourpassword"), // In real-world, use key-based auth
        HostKeyCallback: ssh.InsecureIgnoreHostKey(), // Insecure for demo, use proper host key verification
    }
    client, err := ssh.Dial("tcp", server+":22", config)
    if err != nil {
        return fmt.Errorf("dial failed: %w", err)
    }
    defer client.Close()

    session, err := client.NewSession()
    if err != nil {
        return fmt.Errorf("session failed: %w", err)
    }
    defer session.Close()
```

```go
    // Copy the binary using scp (you can also use sftp or other methods)
    scpCmd := fmt.Sprintf("scp %s %s@%s:/tmp/", binaryPath, user, server)
    scp := exec.Command("sh", "-c", scpCmd)
    output, err := scp.CombinedOutput()

    if err != nil {
        return fmt.Errorf("scp failed: %w\nOutput: %s", err, output)
    }

    // Execute the binary on the remote server
    remoteCmd := fmt.Sprintf("chmod +x /tmp/%s && /tmp/%s", binaryPath[len(binaryPath)-1], binaryPath[len(binaryPath)-1]) // Make executable and run
    cmd := fmt.Sprintf("ssh %s@%s '%s'", user, server, remoteCmd)

    sshExec := exec.Command("sh", "-c", cmd)
    output, err = sshExec.CombinedOutput()

    if err != nil {
        return fmt.Errorf("remote execution failed: %w\nOutput: %s", err, output)
    }

    fmt.Println(string(output))

    return nil
}

func main() {
    server := "yourserver"
    user := "youruser"
    binaryPath := "./mybinary" // Path to your built binary
```

```go
    err := deploy(server, user, binaryPath)
    if err != nil {
        log.Fatal(err)
    }

    fmt.Println("Deployment complete.")
}
```

5. Integrating with CI/CD Systems:

Go is often used to build custom tools or extensions for CI/CD systems like Jenkins, GitLab CI, or GitHub Actions. This allows you to automate the entire build, test, and deployment process.

6. Containerization (Docker and Kubernetes):

Docker and Kubernetes are essential for modern deployments. Go can be used to build tools that interact with Docker and Kubernetes APIs to automate container builds, deployments, and management.

7. Cloud-Specific Deployment Tools:

Cloud providers offer Go SDKs that can be used to automate deployments to their platforms. This includes deploying to services like AWS ECS, Google Cloud Run, or Azure Kubernetes Service.

8. Configuration Management:

Use configuration management tools like Consul or etcd to store and manage configuration data for your deployments. Go can interact with these tools to retrieve and apply the necessary configuration.

9. Best Practices:

Idempotency: Design your deployments to be idempotent, so they can be run multiple times without causing unintended side effects.

Version Control: Keep your deployment scripts and configuration files in version control.

Testing: Thoroughly test your deployments to ensure they work as expected.

Rollback Strategy: Implement a rollback plan to revert to a previous version if the deployment fails.

Security: Securely manage credentials and access to your deployment environments.

Monitoring: Monitor your deployments and applications to detect any issues.

By combining Go's programming power with the right tools and techniques, you can create highly automated and efficient cloud deployment pipelines. Remember to consult the documentation for the specific tools and cloud providers you are using for more details and examples. This chapter provides a solid foundation for building sophisticated deployment automation solutions with Go.

4.3 Building Reusable Infrastructure Modules in Go

This chapter focuses on building reusable infrastructure modules in Go. While Terraform excels at infrastructure as code, Go can enhance this by creating tools that generate and manage these Terraform configurations dynamically. This approach promotes modularity, reduces code duplication, and simplifies infrastructure management.

1. Understanding the Benefits of Modularization:

Modularizing your infrastructure offers several advantages:

Reusability: Modules can be reused across different projects or environments, saving time and effort.

Maintainability: Changes to a module can be easily propagated to all its users.

Abstraction: Modules hide the complexity of the underlying infrastructure, making it easier for others to use.

Consistency: Modules ensure consistent infrastructure configurations across deployments.

2. Approaches to Building Modules with Go:

Go can be used to create reusable infrastructure modules in a few ways:

Generating Terraform Configuration: Go can generate Terraform configuration files (.tf files) dynamically based on templates and input data. This is a common approach for creating modules with customizable parameters.

Building Custom Terraform Providers: For more complex scenarios, you can build custom Terraform providers using Go. This allows you to manage resources that are not supported by existing providers or to implement custom logic for resource provisioning.

Creating Go Libraries for Infrastructure Management: You can create Go libraries that encapsulate common infrastructure management tasks, such as deploying applications, configuring load balancers, or setting up monitoring. These libraries can then be used by other Go applications or tools.

3. Example: Generating Terraform Configuration with Go Templates:

This example demonstrates how to use Go templates to generate Terraform configuration for a set of servers.

Go
```go
package main

import (
    "fmt"
    "log"
    "os"
    "text/template"
)

type Server struct {
    Name    string
    Size    string
    Region  string
}

func main() {
    servers := []Server{
            {Name: "web-server-1", Size: "t2.medium", Region: "us-east-1"},
            {Name: "db-server-1", Size: "db.t3.micro", Region: "us-west-2"},
    }

    // Create a Terraform template
    tmpl, err := template.New("server.tf").Parse(`
resource "aws_instance" "{{ .Name }}" {
  ami           = "ami-0c94855ba95c574c8" # Replace with your AMI
  instance_type = "{{ .Size }}"
  region        = "{{ .Region }}"
```

```go
  tags = {
    Name = "{{ .Name }}"
  }
}
`)

    if err != nil {
        log.Fatal(err)
    }

    // Generate Terraform configuration for each server
    for _, server := range servers {
        filename := fmt.Sprintf("./modules/%s.tf", server.Name)
        err := generateTerraformFile(filename, tmpl, server)
        if err != nil {
                log.Fatalf("Error generating Terraform file for %s: %v",
server.Name, err)
        }
            fmt.Printf("Generated Terraform configuration for %s\n",
server.Name)
    }

    fmt.Println("Terraform configuration generation complete.")
}

func        generateTerraformFile(filename        string,        tmpl
*template.Template, data interface{}) error {
    f, err := os.Create(filename)
    if err != nil {
        return fmt.Errorf("error creating file: %w", err)
    }
    defer f.Close()

    err = tmpl.Execute(f, data)
```

```go
    if err != nil {
        return fmt.Errorf("error executing template: %w", err)
    }
    return nil
}
```

4. Building Reusable Go Libraries:

You can create Go packages that encapsulate common infrastructure management tasks. These packages can then be imported and used by other Go applications or tools.

Go
```go
package infra

import (
    "fmt"
    // ... other imports
)

// Function to deploy an application to a server
func DeployApplication(server, appPath string) error {
    // ... logic to deploy the application (e.g., using SSH, Docker, etc.)
    fmt.Printf("Deploying %s to %s\n", appPath, server)
    return nil
}

// Function to configure a load balancer
func ConfigureLoadBalancer(lbName string, servers []string) error {
    // ... logic to configure the load balancer (e.g., using cloud provider SDK)
    fmt.Printf("Configuring load balancer %s\n", lbName)
```

```
    return nil
}
```

5. Integrating with Configuration Management:

Use configuration management tools like Consul or etcd to store
and manage configuration data for your infrastructure modules. Go
can interact with these tools to retrieve and apply the necessary
configuration.

6. Versioning and Publishing Modules:

Use Git and a package manager (e.g., Go modules) to version and
publish your infrastructure modules. This makes it easier to share
and reuse them across projects.

7. Best Practices:

Well-Defined Interfaces: Define clear and consistent interfaces
for your modules.

Documentation: Document your modules thoroughly, including
their inputs, outputs, and usage instructions.

Testing: Test your modules thoroughly to ensure they work as
expected.

Idempotency: Design your modules to be idempotent, so they can
be run multiple times without causing unintended side effects.

Security: Securely manage any credentials or sensitive
information used by your modules.

By building reusable infrastructure modules with Go, you can
significantly improve the efficiency and maintainability of your
infrastructure management workflows. Go's flexibility and powerful
features make it an excellent choice for creating tools that

enhance and extend your infrastructure as code practices. Remember to install any required Go packages using `go get`.

Chapter 5

Configuration Management with Go

5.1 Automating Server Configuration with Go

This chapter explores automating server configuration using Go. We'll cover various techniques and tools for managing server configurations, from simple configuration file management to more advanced approaches using configuration management systems.

1. Configuration File Management:

Go's standard library provides tools for working with configuration files in various formats (JSON, YAML, TOML, etc.). This is a basic approach suitable for simpler configurations.

```go
Go
package main

import (
    "encoding/json"
    "fmt"
    "io/ioutil"
    "log"
)

type Config struct {
    Server struct {
        Host string `json:"host"`
        Port int    `json:"port"`
    } `json:"server"`
    Database struct {
        User     string `json:"user"`
        Password string `json:"password"`
```

```go
    } `json:"database"`
}

func loadConfig(filename string) (*Config, error) {
    data, err := ioutil.ReadFile(filename)
    if err != nil {
        return nil, fmt.Errorf("error reading config file: %w", err)
    }

    var config Config
    err = json.Unmarshal(data, &config)
    if err != nil {
        return nil, fmt.Errorf("error unmarshalling config: %w", err)
    }

    return &config, nil
}

func main() {
    config, err := loadConfig("config.json")
    if err != nil {
        log.Fatal(err)
    }

    fmt.Println("Server Host:", config.Server.Host)
    fmt.Println("Server Port:", config.Server.Port)
    fmt.Println("Database User:", config.Database.User)
    fmt.Println("Database Password:", config.Database.Password)

    // ... use the configuration data ...
}
```

2. SSH and Remote Command Execution:

Go's `crypto/ssh` package allows you to connect to remote servers and execute commands. This is useful for automating server configuration tasks.

Go
```go
package main

import (
   "fmt"
   "log"
   "golang.org/x/crypto/ssh"
)

func runCommand(server, user, command string) (string, error) {
   config := &ssh.ClientConfig{
      User: user,
         Auth: &ssh.Password("yourpassword"), // In real-world, use key-based auth
         HostKeyCallback: ssh.InsecureIgnoreHostKey(), // Insecure for demo, use proper host key verification
   }
   client, err := ssh.Dial("tcp", server+":22", config)
   if err != nil {
      return "", fmt.Errorf("dial failed: %w", err)
   }
   defer client.Close()

   session, err := client.NewSession()
   if err != nil {
      return "", fmt.Errorf("session failed: %w", err)
   }
   defer session.Close()

   output, err := session.CombinedOutput([]byte(command))
```

```go
    if err != nil {
        return "", fmt.Errorf("command failed: %w\nOutput: %s", err,
output)
    }

    return string(output), nil
}

func main() {
    server := "yourserver"
    user := "youruser"
    command := "ls -l /tmp"

    output, err := runCommand(server, user, command)
    if err != nil {
        log.Fatal(err)
    }

    fmt.Println(output)
}
```

3. Configuration Management Systems (Ansible, Chef, Puppet):

While Go can be used to interact with configuration files and execute commands, dedicated configuration management systems (CMS) like Ansible, Chef, or Puppet offer more advanced features:

Idempotency: CMS ensure that configurations are applied consistently, even if they are run multiple times.

Declarative Configuration: You define the desired state of your servers, and the CMS takes care of achieving that state.

Centralized Management: CMS provide a central platform for managing and monitoring server configurations.

Go can be used to integrate with these CMS through their APIs or command-line tools.

4. Example: Interacting with Ansible from Go:

```go
Go
package main

import (
    "fmt"
    "log"
    "os/exec"
)

func runAnsiblePlaybook(playbookPath string) error {
    cmd := exec.Command("ansible-playbook", playbookPath)
    output, err := cmd.CombinedOutput()
    if err != nil {
        return fmt.Errorf("ansible-playbook failed: %w\nOutput: %s", err, output)
    }
    fmt.Println(string(output))
    return nil
}

func main() {
    playbookPath := "./my-ansible-playbook.yml"
    err := runAnsiblePlaybook(playbookPath)
    if err != nil {
        log.Fatal(err)
    }
    fmt.Println("Ansible playbook execution complete.")
}
```

5. Cloud-Init and Metadata:

Cloud providers often offer cloud-init or metadata services that allow you to configure servers during instance startup. Go can be used to generate cloud-init configurations or retrieve metadata information.

6. Containers and Orchestration (Docker, Kubernetes):

For containerized applications, configuration is often handled through Dockerfiles, Kubernetes ConfigMaps, and Secrets. Go can be used to generate and manage these configurations.

7. Best Practices:

Version Control: Keep your configuration files and automation scripts in version control.

Idempotency: Design your configuration management to be idempotent.

Testing: Test your server configurations thoroughly.

Security: Securely manage credentials and access to your servers.

Monitoring: Monitor your server configurations to detect any issues.

Automating server configuration is crucial for efficient and consistent infrastructure management. Go provides the tools and flexibility to integrate with various configuration management systems and build custom automation solutions. Remember to install any required Go packages using go get. Choose the approach that best suits your needs, from simple configuration files to advanced configuration management systems.

5.2 Managing System State with Go and Ansible/Chef/Puppet (or a custom tool)

This chapter explores how to manage system state using Go in conjunction with configuration management systems (CMS) like Ansible, Chef, or Puppet, or by building a custom tool. We'll examine the benefits of each approach and provide examples to help you choose the best solution for your needs.

1. Understanding System State:

System state refers to the current configuration and status of a system, including installed software, configuration files, running services, and other relevant parameters. Managing system state ensures consistency, reduces configuration drift, and simplifies troubleshooting.

2. Configuration Management Systems (CMS):

CMS like Ansible, Chef, and Puppet are designed specifically for managing system state. They offer features like:

Declarative Configuration: You define the desired state of your systems, and the CMS takes care of achieving that state.

Idempotency: Configurations can be applied multiple times without causing unintended side effects.

Centralized Management: CMS provide a central platform for managing and monitoring system configurations.

3. Integrating Go with CMS:

Go can be used to enhance and extend the capabilities of CMS:

Dynamic Configuration Generation: Go can generate configuration files for CMS dynamically based on templates, databases, or other data sources.

Custom Modules/Plugins: You can develop custom modules or plugins for CMS using Go to manage resources or perform actions not supported by existing modules.

Orchestration and Automation: Go can be used to orchestrate complex workflows involving CMS, such as provisioning infrastructure, applying configurations, and running tests.

4. Example: Dynamic Ansible Inventory Generation with Go:

```go
Go
package main

import (
    "fmt"
    "log"
    "os"
    "text/template"
)

type Server struct {
    Name    string
    IP      string
    Group   string
}

func main() {
    servers := []Server{
            {Name: "web-server-1", IP: "192.168.1.10", Group: "webservers"},
            {Name: "db-server-1", IP: "192.168.1.20", Group: "dbservers"},
```

```go
    }

    // Create an Ansible inventory template
    tmpl, err := template.New("inventory.ini").Parse(`
[{{ .Group }}]
{{ .Name }} ansible_host={{ .IP }}

[all:vars]
ansible_user=youruser
ansible_ssh_private_key_file=~/.ssh/your_private_key
`)

    if err != nil {
        log.Fatal(err)
    }

    // Generate Ansible inventory file
    f, err := os.Create("./inventory.ini")
    if err != nil {
        log.Fatal(err)
    }
    defer f.Close()

    for _, server := range servers {
        err := tmpl.Execute(f, server)
        if err != nil {
            log.Fatal(err)
        }
    }

    fmt.Println("Ansible inventory file generated.")

    // ... (Then run Ansible playbooks using this inventory)
}
```

5. Building a Custom System State Management Tool with Go:

For specific use cases, building a custom system state management tool with Go might be preferable. This gives you complete control over the tool's functionality and allows you to tailor it precisely to your needs.

Advantages:

Flexibility: You can implement any logic or feature you require.

Integration: You can easily integrate your tool with other systems or APIs.

Performance: Go's performance can be beneficial for managing large numbers of systems.

Disadvantages:

Development Effort: Building a custom tool requires significant development effort.

Maintenance: You are responsible for maintaining the tool.

6. Example: Simple Custom System State Checker:

```Go
package main

import (
    "fmt"
    "log"
    "os/exec"
)

type System struct {
```

```go
    Name    string
    Checks  []string // Commands to check system state
}

func checkSystemState(system System) {
    fmt.Printf("Checking system state for %s:\n", system.Name)
    for _, check := range system.Checks {
        cmd := exec.Command("sh", "-c", check)
        output, err := cmd.CombinedOutput()
        if err != nil {
            log.Printf("Check '%s' failed: %v\nOutput: %s", check, err,
output)
        } else {
            fmt.Printf("Check '%s' OK:\n%s", check, output)
        }
    }
}

func main() {
    systems := []System{
        {
            Name: "web-server-1",
            Checks: []string{
                "systemctl status nginx",
                "ps aux | grep myapp",
            },
        },
        {
            Name: "db-server-1",
            Checks: []string{
                "systemctl status postgresql",
                "df -h",
            },
        },
    }
```

```
    for _, system := range systems {
        checkSystemState(system)
    }
}
```

7. Choosing the Right Approach:

Use a CMS (Ansible, Chef, Puppet): If you need to manage a large number of systems with complex configurations and require features like idempotency, declarative configuration, and centralized management.

Use Go with a CMS: If you need to extend the capabilities of a CMS with custom logic, dynamic configuration generation, or integration with other systems.

Build a custom tool with Go: If you have very specific requirements that are not met by existing CMS and you need complete control over the tool's functionality.

8. Best Practices:

Version Control: Keep your configuration files and automation scripts in version control.

Testing: Test your system state management thoroughly.

Security: Securely manage credentials and access to your systems.

Monitoring: Monitor the state of your systems to detect any issues.

Managing system state effectively is crucial for reliable and consistent infrastructure operations. Choose the approach that best suits your needs and remember to follow best practices for version control, testing, security, and monitoring. Remember to install any required Go packages using `go get`.

5.3 Building Configuration Management Tools in Go

This chapter delves into building configuration management tools (CMTs) using Go. While established tools like Ansible, Chef, and Puppet exist, building custom CMTs with Go can be advantageous for specific needs, offering flexibility, performance, and deep integration capabilities.

1. Understanding Configuration Management Principles:

Before building, it's essential to grasp core configuration management principles:

Declarative vs. Imperative: Declarative configuration defines the *desired state*, while imperative specifies the *steps* to achieve it. Go CMTs can implement either approach.

Idempotency: Running a configuration action multiple times has the same effect as running it once. This is crucial for reliable automation.

Version Control: Configuration code should be versioned just like application code.

Testing: Automated testing is crucial for ensuring configuration correctness.

2. Core Components of a Go CMT:

A typical Go CMT might consist of:

Configuration Parser: Reads configuration files (YAML, JSON, TOML, etc.) defining the desired system state. Go's `encoding/json`, `gopkg.in/yaml.v3`, and other libraries handle this.

State Store: Stores the current state of managed systems. This could be a local file, a database, or a distributed key-value store (etcd, Consul).

Action Executor: Executes actions to bring systems to the desired state. This might involve SSH commands, API calls, or interaction with system services.

Diff Engine: Compares the desired state with the current state to determine what actions need to be taken.

Reporting and Logging: Provides information about the configuration process, including successes, failures, and changes.

3. Example: A Basic File Management CMT:

This example demonstrates a simple CMT that manages files on remote servers.

Go
```
package main

import (
    "fmt"
    "io/ioutil"
    "log"
    "os"
    "os/exec"
    "text/template"

    "golang.org/x/crypto/ssh"
    "gopkg.in/yaml.v3"
```

```go
)

type File struct {
    Path    string `yaml:"path"`
    Content string `yaml:"content"`
    Mode    string `yaml:"mode"` // e.g., "0644"
}

type Server struct {
    Host    string `yaml:"host"`
    User    string `yaml:"user"`
    Files   []File `yaml:"files"`
}

type Config struct {
    Servers []Server `yaml:"servers"`
}

func loadConfig(filename string) (*Config, error) {
    // ... (same as previous examples)
}


func applyFileConfig(server Server, file File) error {
    // 1. Check if the file exists and has the correct content and
    mode
    // ... (use SSH to execute commands like 'stat', 'cat')

    // 2. If the file is missing or incorrect, create/update it
    // ... (use SSH and 'scp' or 'echo' redirection to create/update
    the file)

    // Example using SSH and a template for content:
    tmpl, err := template.New("file-content").Parse(file.Content)
    if err != nil {
```

```go
            return err
    }

    // Execute template and write to temporary file
    tempFile, err := ioutil.TempFile("", "config-")
    if err != nil {
            return err
    }
    defer os.Remove(tempFile.Name())
     err = tmpl.Execute(tempFile, nil) // Pass any necessary data
to the template
    if err != nil {
            return err
    }

    // ... (Use scp to copy tempFile to the remote server)
                scpCmd := fmt.Sprintf("scp %s %s@%s:%s",
tempFile.Name(), server.User, server.Host, file.Path)
    scp := exec.Command("sh", "-c", scpCmd)
    output, err := scp.CombinedOutput()

    if err != nil {
        return fmt.Errorf("scp failed: %w\nOutput: %s", err, output)
    }

    // ... (Use SSH to set file permissions if necessary)
     chmodCmd := fmt.Sprintf("ssh %s@%s 'chmod %s %s'",
server.User, server.Host, file.Mode, file.Path)
    chmodExec := exec.Command("sh", "-c", chmodCmd)
    output, err = chmodExec.CombinedOutput()

    if err != nil {
        return fmt.Errorf("chmod failed: %w\nOutput: %s", err, output)
    }
```

```go
        return nil
}

func main() {
        config, err := loadConfig("config.yaml")
        if err != nil {
                log.Fatal(err)
        }

        for _, server := range config.Servers {
                for _, file := range server.Files {
                        err := applyFileConfig(server, file)
                        if err != nil {
                                log.Printf("Error configuring %s:%s - %v",
server.Host, file.Path, err)
                        }
                }
        }
}
```

4. Advanced Features:

Dependency Management: Handle dependencies between configuration actions (e.g., service must be installed before it can be configured).

Templating: Use Go's `text/template` package for templating configuration files.

Rollback: Implement rollback mechanisms to revert changes if necessary.

Parallel Execution: Use Go's concurrency features to apply configurations to multiple servers concurrently.

API Integration: Integrate with cloud provider APIs or other services.

5. Choosing the Right Approach:

Use an existing CMS: If your needs are well-covered by existing tools and you value their features and community support.

Build a custom CMT: If you have very specific requirements, need deep integration with other systems, or want to optimize for performance in a particular way.

6. Best Practices:

Modularity: Break down your configuration into reusable modules or components.

Testing: Write unit and integration tests for your CMT.

Version Control: Store your configuration code and CMT in version control.

Security: Securely manage credentials and access to your servers.

Documentation: Document your CMT and its usage.

Building a configuration management tool is a complex undertaking. Start with a small set of features and gradually add more as needed. Careful planning, testing, and adherence to best practices are crucial for success. Remember to install any required Go packages using `go get`.

Chapter 6

Containerization with Go and Docker

6.1 Building and Managing Docker Images with Go

This chapter focuses on building and managing Docker images using Go. We'll explore how to programmatically interact with the Docker daemon to build images, manage containers, and automate Docker-related workflows.

1. Interacting with the Docker Daemon:

Go provides a Docker client library (`github.com/docker/docker/client`) that allows you to interact with the Docker daemon programmatically. This library provides functions for all common Docker operations.

2. Example: Building a Docker Image from a Dockerfile:

Go
```
package main

import (
    "context"
    "fmt"
    "io"
    "log"
    "os"

    "github.com/docker/docker/api/types"
    "github.com/docker/docker/client"
```

```go
)

func main() {
    ctx := context.Background()
    cli, err := client.NewClientWithOpts(client.FromEnv,
client.WithAPIVersionNegotiation())
    if err != nil {
        log.Fatal(err)
    }
    defer cli.Close()

    dockerfile := "./Dockerfile" // Path to your Dockerfile
    buildCtx, err := os.Open(dockerfile)
    if err != nil {
        log.Fatal(err)
    }
    defer buildCtx.Close()

    buildResponse, err := cli.ImageBuild(ctx, buildCtx,
types.ImageBuildOptions{
        Tags: []string{"my-go-image:latest"}, // Image tag
    })
    if err != nil {
        log.Fatal(err)
    }
    defer buildResponse.Body.Close()

    // Print build output (optional)
    _, err = io.Copy(os.Stdout, buildResponse.Body)
    if err != nil {
        log.Println("Error copying build output:", err) // Don't
Fatal on this
    }

    fmt.Println("Docker image built successfully.")
```

}

3. Example: Pulling a Docker Image:

Go
```
// ... (client setup as in the previous example)

pullResponse, err := cli.ImagePull(ctx, "nginx:latest",
types.ImagePullOptions{})
if err != nil {
    log.Fatal(err)
}
defer pullResponse.Close()

io.Copy(os.Stdout, pullResponse) // Print pull progress
fmt.Println("Image pulled successfully.")
```

4. Example: Running a Docker Container:

Go
```
// ... (client setup as in the previous example)

resp, err := cli.ContainerCreate(ctx, &docker.Config{
    Image: "my-go-image:latest",
    ExposedPorts: nat.PortSet{
        "8080/tcp": struct{}{},
    },
}, &docker.HostConfig{
    PortBindings: nat.PortMap{
        "8080/tcp": []nat.PortBinding{
            {
                HostIP:   "0.0.0.0",
                HostPort: "8080",
```

```
        },
      },
    },
  },
}, nil, nil, "my-go-container")

if err != nil {
    log.Fatal(err)
}

err = cli.ContainerStart(ctx, resp.ID, types.ContainerStartOptions{})
if err != nil {
    log.Fatal(err)
}

fmt.Println("Container started successfully.")

// ... (You can then use cli.ContainerInspect, cli.ContainerStop, etc.
to manage the container)
```

5. Docker Compose:

For multi-container applications, you can use Go to interact with Docker Compose. While there isn't an official Go library specifically for Docker Compose, you can use the os/exec package to run Docker Compose commands.

Go
```
cmd := exec.Command("docker-compose", "up", "-d") // Example:
start containers in detached mode
output, err := cmd.CombinedOutput()
// ... (Handle errors and output)
```

6. Building Multi-Stage Dockerfiles:

Go is often used in multi-stage Docker builds. The first stage compiles the Go application, and the second (smaller) stage copies the compiled binary into a minimal base image. This reduces the final image size.

7. Integrating with CI/CD:

Go is well-suited for building tools that automate Docker builds and deployments in CI/CD pipelines. This could involve building images, pushing them to registries, and deploying them to container orchestration platforms like Kubernetes.

8. Best Practices:

Use a `.dockerignore` **file:** Exclude unnecessary files from your Docker image build context to reduce image size and build time.

Multi-stage builds: Use multi-stage builds to create smaller and more efficient images.

Image tagging: Use meaningful tags for your Docker images (e.g., version numbers, commit hashes).

Security: Securely manage Docker credentials and access to your Docker registry.

Testing: Test your Docker images thoroughly.

By combining Go's programming power with the Docker client library, you can create sophisticated tools and automation workflows for building, managing, and deploying Docker images. Remember to install the Docker client library using `go get` `github.com/docker/docker/client` and the `github.com/docker/go-connections/nat` package for port mappings. This chapter provides a solid foundation for working with Docker in your Go applications.

6.2 Orchestrating Containers with Docker Compose and Go

This chapter explores how to orchestrate containers using Docker Compose and Go. While Docker Compose is a powerful tool on its own, combining it with Go allows for more dynamic and programmatic control over your containerized applications.

1. Understanding Docker Compose:

Docker Compose is a tool for defining and running multi-container Docker applications. It uses a YAML file (`docker-compose.yml`) to define the services[1] (containers) that make up your application, their dependencies, and their configurations.

2. Interacting with Docker Compose from Go:

Go doesn't have a dedicated, official library specifically for Docker Compose like it does for the Docker daemon itself. The most common and effective approach is to use Go's `os/exec` package to execute Docker Compose commands.

3. Example: Running Docker Compose Commands:

Go
```
package main

import (
    "fmt"
    "log"
    "os/exec"
)
```

```go
func runDockerComposeCommand(command string, composeFile string) (string, error) {
    cmd := exec.Command("docker-compose", "-f", composeFile, command) // -f specifies the compose file
    output, err := cmd.CombinedOutput()
    if err != nil {
        return "", fmt.Errorf("docker-compose %s failed: %w\nOutput: %s", command, err, output)
    }
    return string(output), nil
}

func main() {
    composeFile := "./docker-compose.yml" // Path to your docker-compose.yml file

    // Example: Running 'docker-compose up -d'
    output, err := runDockerComposeCommand("up -d", composeFile)
    if err != nil {
        log.Fatal(err)
    }
    fmt.Println(output)

    // Example: Running 'docker-compose down'
    output, err = runDockerComposeCommand("down", composeFile)
    if err != nil {
        log.Fatal(err)
    }
    fmt.Println(output)

    //Example: Running 'docker-compose ps'
    output, err = runDockerComposeCommand("ps", composeFile)
```

```go
    if err != nil {
        log.Fatal(err)
    }
    fmt.Println(output)


}
```

4. Advanced Scenarios:

Dynamic Compose File Generation: Go can be used to generate `docker-compose.yml` files dynamically based on configuration data, environment variables, or other inputs. This is useful for creating flexible and customizable deployments. You can use Go's `text/template` package for this, as shown in previous chapters.

Orchestrating Complex Deployments: Go can orchestrate complex deployments involving multiple Docker Compose files or interactions with other tools.

Integrating with Cloud Platforms: Go can be used to build tools that deploy and manage Docker Compose applications on cloud platforms like AWS ECS, Google Cloud Run, or Azure Container Instances.

CI/CD Integration: Go can be integrated with CI/CD systems to automate the deployment of Docker Compose applications.

5. Example: Dynamic Compose File Generation with Go Templates:

```go
Go
package main

import (
```

```go
    "fmt"
    "log"
    "os"
    "text/template"
)

type Service struct {
    Name  string
    Image string
    Port  string
}

func main() {
    services := []Service{
        {Name: "web", Image: "nginx:latest", Port: "80:80"},
        {Name: "db", Image: "postgres:latest", Port: "5432:5432"},
    }

    tmpl, err := template.New("docker-compose.yml").Parse(`
version: "3.8"
services:
{{ range . }}
  {{ .Name }}:
    image: {{ .Image }}
    ports:
      - "{{ .Port }}"
{{ end }}
`)

    if err != nil {
        log.Fatal(err)
    }

    f, err := os.Create("./docker-compose.yml")
    if err != nil {
```

```
    log.Fatal(err)
}
defer f.Close()

err = tmpl.Execute(f, services)
if err != nil {
    log.Fatal(err)
}

fmt.Println("docker-compose.yml generated.")

// ... (Then run docker-compose commands as in the previous
example)
}
```

6. Best Practices:

Version Control: Keep your `docker-compose.yml` files and Go scripts in version control.

Testing: Test your Docker Compose deployments thoroughly.

Configuration Management: Use environment variables or configuration management tools to manage configuration data for your Docker Compose applications.

Logging and Monitoring: Implement logging and monitoring for your Docker Compose applications.

By combining Docker Compose with Go, you can create powerful and flexible solutions for managing multi-container applications. Go provides the programming power to dynamically generate configurations, orchestrate complex deployments, and integrate with other tools and systems. This chapter provides a solid foundation for working with Docker Compose and Go. Remember to have Docker and Docker Compose installed on your system.

6.3 Go for Containerized Application Development

This chapter explores using Go for developing containerized applications, focusing on best practices, common patterns, and tools that enhance the development workflow for cloud-native environments.

1. Why Go and Containers are a Great Match:

Go's strengths align perfectly with containerization:

Static Linking: Go compiles to a single binary, simplifying container images and reducing their size. No runtime dependencies are needed in the final image (other than perhaps `libc` itself).

Performance: Go's performance is excellent, making it suitable for building high-throughput services within containers.

Concurrency: Go's built-in concurrency features (goroutines and channels) are ideal for building scalable and responsive applications that thrive in containerized environments.

Small Footprint: Go binaries are relatively small, contributing to smaller container image sizes, which translates to faster deployments and less resource consumption.

Cross-Compilation: Go's cross-compilation capabilities make it easy to build binaries for different target platforms directly from your development environment.

2. Structuring Your Go Application for Containers:

Single Binary: Design your Go application to be contained within a single binary. This simplifies the Dockerfile and reduces image layers.

Configuration from Environment Variables: Use environment variables to inject configuration into your application. This is a best practice for containerized applications as it allows you to easily change configurations without rebuilding the image.

Graceful Shutdown: Implement graceful shutdown handling in your Go application. This allows your application to cleanly exit when the container is stopped or terminated, preventing data loss and ensuring a smooth transition. Use signals (`os.Signal`) to trap termination requests.

Health Checks: Expose a health check endpoint in your application. Container orchestrators like Kubernetes use health checks to determine if your application is running correctly. This can be a simple HTTP endpoint that returns a 200 OK status.

Logging: Use structured logging (e.g., JSON format) to make it easier to collect and analyze logs from your containerized applications. Consider using a logging library like `logrus` or `zap`.

Metrics: Expose metrics about your application's performance (e.g., request latency, memory usage) using a library like Prometheus client. This allows you to monitor your application's health and performance in a containerized environment.

3. Example: A Basic Go Web Server for Containers:

```go
Go
package main

import (
```

```go
    "context"
    "fmt"
    "log"
    "net/http"
    "os"
    "os/signal"
    "syscall"
    "time"
)

func main() {
    port := os.Getenv("PORT")
    if port == "" {
        port = "8080"
    }

    http.HandleFunc("/", func(w http.ResponseWriter, r *http.Request) {
        fmt.Fprintln(w, "Hello from Go in a container!")
    })

    server := &http.Server{
        Addr:    ":" + port,
        Handler: http.DefaultServeMux,
    }

    go func() {
        if err := server.ListenAndServe(); err != http.ErrServerClosed {
            log.Fatalf("Server stopped unexpectedly: %v", err)
        }
    }()

    fmt.Printf("Server listening on port %s\n", port)
```

```go
    // Graceful shutdown
    quit := make(chan os.Signal, 1)
    signal.Notify(quit, syscall.SIGINT, syscall.SIGTERM)
    <-quit

    fmt.Println("Shutting down server...")

        ctx, cancel := context.WithTimeout(context.Background(),
5*time.Second)
    defer cancel()

    if err := server.Shutdown(ctx); err != nil {
        log.Fatalf("Server shutdown failed: %v", err)
    }

    fmt.Println("Server gracefully stopped.")
}
```

4. Dockerfile Best Practices:

Use a Minimal Base Image: Start with a small base image (e.g., scratch, alpine) to reduce the size of your final image. If you need some standard tooling, a slim variant of a distribution (like debian-slim) might be a good choice.

Multi-Stage Builds: Use multi-stage builds to compile your Go application in one stage and then copy the binary to a smaller image in a later stage. This reduces the final image size.

Don't Install Unnecessary Packages: Only install the packages that are absolutely required for your application to run.

Use .dockerignore: Create a .dockerignore file to exclude unnecessary files and directories from your image build context.

Non-root User: Run your application as a non-root user for security best practices.

5. Example Dockerfile (Multi-Stage):

Dockerfile
Build stage
FROM golang:1.20-alpine AS builder

WORKDIR /app

COPY go.mod go.sum ./
RUN go mod download

COPY . .
RUN go build -o myapp

Final stage
FROM scratch

COPY --from=builder /app/myapp /app/myapp

EXPOSE 8080

USER nonroot # Create a nonroot user

ENTRYPOINT ["/app/myapp"]

6. Container Orchestration (Kubernetes):

Go applications are commonly deployed and managed using Kubernetes. You can use Kubernetes deployments, services, and other resources to manage your containerized Go applications.

7. Tools and Libraries:

Go Modules: Use Go modules for dependency management.

Docker Client: Use the official Go Docker client library (`github.com/docker/docker/client`) for interacting with the Docker daemon.

Prometheus Client: Use the Prometheus Go client library (`github.com/prometheus/client_golang`) for instrumenting your application with metrics.

Logging Libraries: Use a structured logging library like `logrus` or `zap`.

8. Best Practices:

Immutable Infrastructure: Treat your containers as immutable. Deploy new containers instead of modifying existing ones.

Continuous Integration/Continuous Deployment (CI/CD): Integrate your container builds and deployments into a CI/CD pipeline.

Monitoring and Logging: Implement robust monitoring and logging for your containerized applications.

Security: Follow security best practices for containerized applications.

By following these best practices and using the appropriate tools, you can effectively develop and deploy Go applications in containerized environments. Go's strengths make it an excellent choice for building cloud-native applications that are performant, scalable, and easy to manage.

Chapter 7

Orchestration with Go and Kubernetes

7.1 Deploying and Managing Applications on Kubernetes with Go

This chapter explores deploying and managing applications on Kubernetes using Go. We'll cover how to build Go applications specifically for Kubernetes, interact with the Kubernetes API, and use tools and libraries that simplify Kubernetes deployments and management.

1. Building Go Applications for Kubernetes:

Health Checks: Implement health check endpoints in your Go applications. Kubernetes uses these endpoints to determine if your application is running correctly. Liveness probes check if a container is still running, while readiness probes check if it's ready to serve traffic.

Graceful Shutdown: Implement graceful shutdown handling to allow your application to cleanly exit when the pod is terminated. This prevents data loss and ensures a smooth transition.

Configuration from ConfigMaps and Secrets: Use Kubernetes ConfigMaps to store non-sensitive configuration data and Secrets for sensitive information (passwords, API keys). Your Go application can then read this configuration from environment variables or files mounted from ConfigMaps and Secrets.

Logging: Use structured logging (e.g., JSON format) for easy log collection and analysis.

Metrics: Expose metrics using a library like the Prometheus Go client. This allows you to monitor your application's performance in Kubernetes.

2. Example: Go Web Server with Health Check and Configuration:

Go
```go
package main

import (
    "context"
    "fmt"
    "log"
    "net/http"
    "os"
    "os/signal"
    "syscall"
    "time"
)

func main() {
    port := os.Getenv("PORT")
    if port == "" {
        port = "8080"
    }

    // Configuration from environment variables (set by ConfigMap/Secret)
    dbUser := os.Getenv("DB_USER")
    dbPass := os.Getenv("DB_PASSWORD")

    http.HandleFunc("/", func(w http.ResponseWriter, r *http.Request) {
        fmt.Fprintf(w, "Hello from Go in Kubernetes! DB User: %s\n", dbUser)
```

```go
    })

    // Health check endpoint
    http.HandleFunc("/healthz", func(w http.ResponseWriter, r *http.Request) {
        if dbPass == "" { // Simulate a database connection check
            http.Error(w, "Database not ready", http.StatusInternalServerError)
            return
        }
        w.WriteHeader(http.StatusOK)
    })

    server := &http.Server{
        Addr:    ":" + port,
        Handler: http.DefaultServeMux,
    }

    go func() {
        if err := server.ListenAndServe(); err != http.ErrServerClosed {
            log.Fatalf("Server stopped unexpectedly: %v", err)
        }
    }()

    fmt.Printf("Server listening on port %s\n", port)

    // Graceful shutdown
    quit := make(chan os.Signal, 1)
    signal.Notify(quit, syscall.SIGINT, syscall.SIGTERM)
    <-quit

    fmt.Println("Shutting down server...")

    ctx, cancel := context.WithTimeout(context.Background(), 5*time.Second)
```

```go
    defer cancel()

    if err := server.Shutdown(ctx); err != nil {
        log.Fatalf("Server shutdown failed: %v", err)
    }

    fmt.Println("Server gracefully stopped.")
}
```

3. Interacting with the Kubernetes API:

Go provides a client library (`k8s.io/client-go`) for interacting with the Kubernetes API. This allows you to programmatically manage Kubernetes resources (pods, deployments, services, etc.).

4. Example: Listing Pods in a Namespace:

```go
Go
package main

import (
    "context"
    "fmt"
    "log"

    v1 "k8s.io/api/core/v1"
    metav1 "k8s.io/apimachinery/pkg/apis/meta/v1"
    "k8s.io/client-go/kubernetes"
    "k8s.io/client-go/rest"
)

func main() {
    // Creates the in-cluster config
```

```go
    config, err := rest.InClusterConfig()
    if err != nil {
        log.Fatalf("Failed to create in-cluster config: %v", err)
    }

    // Creates the clientSet
    clientset, err := kubernetes.NewForConfig(config)
    if err != nil {
        log.Fatalf("Failed to create clientset: %v", err)
    }

    pods, err := clientset.CoreV1().Pods("default").List(context.TODO(),
metav1.ListOptions{})
    if err != nil {
        log.Fatalf("Failed to list pods: %v", err)
    }

    fmt.Printf("There are %d pods in the default namespace\n",
len(pods.Items))

    for _, pod := range pods.Items {
        fmt.Printf("Pod Name: %s\n", pod.Name)
    }
}
```

5. Kubernetes Controllers:

Custom Kubernetes controllers are a powerful way to automate complex management tasks. You can build controllers in Go that watch for changes to Kubernetes resources and take actions based on those changes. The Operator SDK simplifies controller development.

6. Tools and Libraries:

`k8s.io/client-go`: The official Go client library for Kubernetes.

`operator-sdk`: A framework for building Kubernetes operators (controllers).

`controller-runtime`: A library for building controllers.

7. Deployment Strategies:

Rolling Updates: Update deployments gradually to minimize downtime. Kubernetes handles this automatically.

Blue/Green Deployments: Use two deployments (blue and green) and switch traffic between them.

Canary Deployments: Deploy to a small subset of pods first and then gradually roll out to the rest.

8. Best Practices:

Resource Limits and Requests: Define resource limits and requests for your pods to ensure they have the necessary resources.

Liveness and Readiness Probes: Implement liveness and readiness probes to allow Kubernetes to monitor the health of your application.

Secrets Management: Use Kubernetes Secrets to store sensitive information.

Namespaces: Organize your Kubernetes resources into namespaces.

Helm: Use Helm to package and deploy your Kubernetes applications.

By leveraging Go's capabilities and the Kubernetes API, you can build powerful tools and automation workflows for deploying, managing, and scaling your applications in Kubernetes. Remember to install the Kubernetes client library using `go get k8s.io/client-go`. This chapter provides a solid foundation for working with Kubernetes and Go.

7.2 Building Kubernetes Operators with Go

This chapter explores building Kubernetes Operators using Go. Operators are a powerful way to extend Kubernetes' functionality and automate complex application management tasks. They leverage custom resources (CRs) and controllers to manage the lifecycle of applications in a declarative way.

1. Understanding Kubernetes Operators:

Operators automate the management of complex applications on Kubernetes. Instead of relying on manual steps or scripts, operators use controllers to watch for changes to custom resources (CRs) that define the desired state of an application. The operator then takes actions to reconcile the current state with the desired state defined in the CR.

2. Core Concepts:

Custom Resources (CRs): Extensions to the Kubernetes API that represent your application or its components. You define the structure of your CRs using Go structs.

Controllers: Programs that watch for changes to CRs and take actions to reconcile the desired state with the actual state. Operators are implemented as controllers.

Operator SDK: A toolkit that simplifies the process of building Kubernetes operators with Go. It provides libraries and tools for generating code, managing dependencies, and deploying your operator.

3. Building an Operator with the Operator SDK:

The Operator SDK simplifies operator development. Here's a general workflow:

Install the Operator SDK: Follow the instructions on the Operator SDK GitHub page.

Initialize a Project: Use the `operator-sdk init` command to create a new operator project.

Define the Custom Resource (CR): Define the Go struct that represents your CR. This struct defines the fields that users will specify when creating instances of your custom resource.

Generate Controller Code: Use the `operator-sdk generate controller` command to generate the basic controller code for your CR.

Implement the Controller Logic: Implement the reconciliation logic in the generated controller code. This logic defines the actions that the operator takes when a CR is created, updated, or deleted.

Build and Deploy the Operator: Use the `operator-sdk build` and `operator-sdk deploy` commands to build and deploy your operator to Kubernetes.

4. Example: A Simple Memcached Operator:

This example outlines the steps to build a basic Memcached operator.

Define the CR:

```go
// api/v1alpha1/memcached_types.go
package v1alpha1

import (
    metav1 "k8s.io/apimachinery/pkg/apis/meta/v1"
)

// MemcachedSpec defines the desired state of Memcached
type MemcachedSpec struct {
    Size int32 `json:"size"`
}

// MemcachedStatus defines the observed state of Memcached
type MemcachedStatus struct {
    Nodes []string `json:"nodes"`
}

// +kubebuilder:object:root=true
// +kubebuilder:subresource:status

// Memcached is the Schema for the memcacheds API
type Memcached struct {
    metav1.TypeMeta   `json:",inline"`
    metav1.ObjectMeta `json:"metadata,omitempty"`

    Spec   MemcachedSpec   `json:"spec,omitempty"`
    Status MemcachedStatus `json:"status,omitempty"`
}

// +kubebuilder:object:root=true

// MemcachedList contains a list of Memcached
```

```go
type MemcachedList struct {
    metav1.TypeMeta `json:",inline"`
    metav1.ListMeta `json:"metadata,omitempty"`

    Items []Memcached `json:"items"`
}

func init() {
    SchemeBuilder.Register(&Memcached{}, &MemcachedList{})
}
```

Implement the Controller Logic:

Go
```go
// controllers/memcached_controller.go
package controllers

// ... (imports)

// Reconcile reads that state of the cluster for a Memcached object
and makes changes based on the state read
// and what is in the Memcached.Spec
// Note:
// The Controller manager will call this Reconcile function to
compare the state specified by
// the Memcached object with the actual state.
// It may do so even when a change to the Memcached object is
not observed immediately.
// For more details, please check:
//
https://book.kubebuilder.io/user-guide/concepts/reconciliation.html
func (r *MemcachedReconciler) Reconcile(ctx context.Context, req
ctrl.Request) (ctrl.Result, error) {
    // ... (get the Memcached object)
```

```
    // 1. Check if the Memcached deployment exists. If not, create it.
      // 2. Check if the Memcached size matches the spec. If not,
update the deployment.
      // 3. Update the Memcached status with the list of Memcached
nodes.

    return ctrl.Result{}, nil
}

// SetupWithManager sets up the controller with the Manager.
func    (r    *MemcachedReconciler)    SetupWithManager(mgr
ctrl.Manager) error {
    return ctrl.NewControllerManagedBy(mgr).
      For(&cachev1alpha1.Memcached{}).
      Complete(r)
}
```

Build and Deploy:

```Bash
operator-sdk build
operator-sdk  deploy  --kubeconfig  ~/.kube/config  --namespace
my-namespace
```

5. Advanced Features:

Custom Logic: Implement any custom logic required to manage your application, such as scaling, backups, or upgrades.

Integration with Other Systems: Integrate with other systems or APIs, such as cloud provider APIs or monitoring tools.

Metrics and Logging: Expose metrics and logs to monitor the operator and the applications it manages.

6. Best Practices:

Testing: Thoroughly test your operator to ensure it works as expected.

Error Handling: Implement robust error handling to prevent your operator from crashing.

Security: Securely manage any credentials or access to your Kubernetes cluster.

Documentation: Document your operator and its usage.

Building Kubernetes operators with Go allows you to automate the management of complex applications on Kubernetes. The Operator SDK simplifies the development process and provides a solid foundation for building robust and reliable operators. Remember to install the Operator SDK and Go before starting. This chapter provides a good starting point; refer to the Operator SDK documentation for more detailed information and advanced features.

7.3 Automating Kubernetes Workloads with Go

This chapter explores automating Kubernetes workloads using Go. We'll delve into techniques for programmatically interacting with the Kubernetes API to manage deployments, services, and other resources, enabling you to build powerful automation tools and workflows.

1. Interacting with the Kubernetes API:

Go's `k8s.io/client-go` library is the primary way to interact with the Kubernetes API from your Go applications. It provides a set of clients and tools for managing Kubernetes resources.

2. Authentication and Configuration:

Before interacting with the API, you need to configure authentication. Common methods include:

In-Cluster Configuration: When your application runs within a Kubernetes pod, it can use the in-cluster configuration to automatically authenticate with the API server.

Kubeconfig File: You can use a kubeconfig file to configure access to your Kubernetes cluster from outside the cluster.

3. Example: Creating a Deployment:

```go
Go
package main

import (
    "context"
    "fmt"
    "log"

    appsv1 "k8s.io/api/apps/v1"
    corev1 "k8s.io/api/core/v1"
    metav1 "k8s.io/apimachinery/pkg/apis/meta/v1"
    "k8s.io/client-go/kubernetes"
    "k8s.io/client-go/rest"
)

func main() {
    // Creates the in-cluster config
    config, err := rest.InClusterConfig()
    if err != nil {
        log.Fatalf("Failed to create in-cluster config: %v", err)
    }
```

```go
// Creates the clientSet
clientset, err := kubernetes.NewForConfig(config)
if err != nil {
   log.Fatalf("Failed to create clientset: %v", err)
}

deploymentsClient := clientset.AppsV1().Deployments("default")

deployment := &appsv1.Deployment{
   ObjectMeta: metav1.ObjectMeta{
      Name: "my-go-deployment",
   },
   Spec: appsv1.DeploymentSpec{
      Replicas: aws.Int32(3),
      Selector: &metav1.LabelSelector{
         MatchLabels: map[string]string{
            "app": "my-go-app",
         },
      },
      Template: corev1.PodTemplateSpec{
         ObjectMeta: metav1.ObjectMeta{
            Labels: map[string]string{
               "app": "my-go-app",
            },
         },
         Spec: corev1.PodSpec{
            Containers: []corev1.Container{
               {
                  Name:  "my-go-container",
                     Image: "my-go-image:latest", // Replace with your image
                  Ports: []corev1.ContainerPort{
                     {
                        ContainerPort: 8080,
                     },
```

```go
                },
              },
            },
          },
        },
      },
    }

    // Create Deployment
    fmt.Println("Creating deployment...")
      result, err := deploymentsClient.Create(context.TODO(),
deployment, metav1.CreateOptions{})
    if err != nil {
      log.Fatalf("Failed to create deployment: %v", err)
    }
                fmt.Printf("Created     deployment     %q.\n",
result.GetObjectMeta().GetName())

    // ... (You can then use deploymentsClient to update, delete, or
list deployments)
}
```

4. Automating Common Tasks:

Go can be used to automate various Kubernetes tasks:

Deployments: Creating, updating, and deleting deployments.

Services: Managing services and service discovery.

Pods: Inspecting pod status and logs.

Scaling: Auto-scaling deployments based on metrics.

Resource Management: Setting resource limits and requests for containers.

Custom Controllers (Operators): Implementing custom logic for managing complex applications (as covered in the previous chapter).

5. Example: Scaling a Deployment:

```go
Go
// ... (clientset setup as in the previous example)

deploymentsClient := clientset.AppsV1().Deployments("default")
deploymentName := "my-go-deployment"

// Get the deployment
deployment, err := deploymentsClient.Get(context.TODO(),
deploymentName, metav1.GetOptions{})
if err != nil {
   log.Fatalf("Failed to get deployment: %v", err)
}

// Update the number of replicas
replicas := int32(5) // Scale to 5 replicas
deployment.Spec.Replicas = &replicas

// Update the deployment
_, err = deploymentsClient.Update(context.TODO(), deployment,
metav1.UpdateOptions{})
if err != nil {
   log.Fatalf("Failed to update deployment: %v", err)
}

fmt.Printf("Scaled deployment %s to %d replicas.\n",
deploymentName, replicas)
```

6. Tools and Libraries:

`k8s.io/client-go`: The official Go client library for Kubernetes.

`operator-sdk`: A framework for building Kubernetes operators.

`controller-runtime`: A library for building controllers.

7. Best Practices:

Error Handling: Implement robust error handling in your automation scripts.

Idempotency: Design your automation to be idempotent, so it can be run multiple times without causing unintended side effects.

Testing: Thoroughly test your automation scripts.

Security: Securely manage credentials and access to your Kubernetes cluster.

Configuration Management: Use ConfigMaps and Secrets to manage configuration data for your applications.

By using Go to automate Kubernetes workloads, you can significantly simplify the management of your containerized applications. Go's performance, concurrency features, and strong Kubernetes integration make it an excellent choice for building powerful and efficient automation tools. Remember to install the Kubernetes client library using `go get k8s.io/client-go`. This chapter provides a good starting point; refer to the Kubernetes documentation for more detailed information and examples.

Chapter 8

Continuous Integration and Continuous Delivery (CI/CD) with Go

8.1 Building CI/CD Pipelines with Go and [Your CI/CD Tool of Choice

This chapter explores building Continuous Integration/Continuous Delivery (CI/CD) pipelines using Go and [Your CI/CD Tool of Choice]. We'll cover how Go can be integrated into various stages of your pipeline, from building and testing applications to deploying them to different environments. This chapter provides a general framework; adapt the specifics to your chosen CI/CD tool.

1. Choosing Your CI/CD Tool:

Many excellent CI/CD tools exist, each with its own strengths. Popular choices include:

GitHub Actions: Integrated with GitHub repositories, offering a seamless experience for projects hosted on GitHub.

GitLab CI/CD: Built into GitLab, providing a comprehensive solution for projects hosted on GitLab.

Jenkins: A highly customizable and extensible open-source server.

CircleCI: A cloud-based platform known for its ease of use.

AWS CodePipeline, Google Cloud Build, Azure DevOps: Cloud-provider specific solutions tightly integrated with their respective ecosystems.

For this chapter, we will provide examples using GitHub Actions, but the principles apply to other CI/CD systems.

2. Go's Role in CI/CD:

Go can play several important roles in your CI/CD pipeline:

Building Applications: Go's compilation speed makes it ideal for building applications quickly in the CI environment.

Testing: Go's testing framework is used to run unit tests, integration tests, and end-to-end tests as part of the pipeline.

Linting and Code Analysis: Go linters (e.g., `golangci-lint`) can be integrated into the pipeline to enforce coding standards and identify potential issues.

Building Docker Images: Go can be used to build Docker images as part of the pipeline.

Deploying to Kubernetes: Go can interact with the Kubernetes API to deploy applications to Kubernetes clusters.

Custom Tooling: Go can be used to create custom tools for specific tasks in your pipeline, such as database migrations, infrastructure provisioning, or release management.

3. Example: CI/CD Pipeline with GitHub Actions:

This example demonstrates a basic CI/CD pipeline using GitHub Actions.

```yaml
# .github/workflows/main.yml
name: Go CI/CD

on:
  push:
```

```yaml
    branches: [ main ]
  pull_request:
    branches: [ main ]

jobs:
  build:
    name: Build and Test
    runs-on: ubuntu-latest

    steps:
      - name: Checkout code
        uses: actions/checkout@v3

      - name: Set up Go
        uses: actions/setup-go@v3
        with:
          go-version: '^1.20' # Or your preferred version

      - name: Build
        run: go build -v ./...

      - name: Test
        run: go test -v ./...

      - name: Lint
        run: golangci-lint run

      - name: Build Docker Image
        run: docker build -t my-go-image:latest .

      - name: Push Docker Image (Optional)
        if: github.event_name == 'push'
        run: |
            docker login -u ${{ secrets.DOCKER_USERNAME }} -p ${{
secrets.DOCKER_PASSWORD }}
```

```
    docker push my-go-image:latest

deploy:
    name: Deploy to Kubernetes
    needs: build
    if: github.event_name == 'push' # Only deploy on pushes to
main
    runs-on: ubuntu-latest
    steps:
        - name: Checkout code
            uses: actions/checkout@v3

        - name: Set up Kubectl
            uses: azure/setup-kubectl@v2
            with:
                version: v1.27.3 # Or your preferred version

        - name: Deploy to Kubernetes
            run: kubectl apply -f deployment.yaml # Your
Kubernetes deployment YAML file
```

4. Key Considerations:

Secrets Management: Store sensitive information (API keys, passwords) as secrets in your CI/CD tool and access them securely in your pipeline. Never hardcode secrets in your code.

Caching: Use caching mechanisms to speed up your builds. Go modules and Docker layers can be cached.

Parallelization: Run tests and other independent tasks in parallel to reduce pipeline execution time.

Artifact Management: Store build artifacts (binaries, Docker images) in a repository (e.g., Docker Hub, cloud provider registry).

Deployment Strategies: Implement different deployment strategies (blue/green, canary, rolling updates) as part of your pipeline.

Rollback: Have a rollback strategy in place to revert to a previous version if a deployment fails

Monitoring and Logging: Integrate your CI/CD pipeline with monitoring and logging systems to track its performance and identify any issues.

5. Example: Deploying to Kubernetes with Go in a CI/CD Pipeline:

Instead of using `kubectl apply` directly in the GitHub Actions workflow, you could create a Go tool that interacts with the Kubernetes API for more complex deployment logic. This tool would be built and included in your Docker image. The CI/CD pipeline would then run this tool to perform the deployment.

6. Best Practices:

Infrastructure as Code (IaC): Manage your infrastructure using IaC tools like Terraform. Integrate IaC into your CI/CD pipeline.

Automated Testing: Implement comprehensive testing at all stages of your pipeline.

Continuous Monitoring: Monitor your applications and infrastructure in production.

Security: Secure your CI/CD pipeline and protect sensitive information.

By combining Go with your chosen CI/CD tool, you can create robust and efficient pipelines that automate the entire software delivery process. Remember to adapt the examples and best practices to your specific needs and the capabilities of your CI/CD tool. This chapter provides a solid foundation for building effective CI/CD pipelines.

8.2 Automating Testing and Deployment with Go

This chapter delves into automating testing and deployment processes using Go. We'll explore how Go's capabilities can be leveraged to build robust testing frameworks and create efficient deployment pipelines, enabling continuous integration and continuous delivery (CI/CD).

Part 1: Automating Testing with Go

1. Go's Built-in Testing Framework:

Go provides a built-in testing framework through the `testing` package. It's simple yet powerful, allowing you to write unit tests, benchmark tests, and example-based documentation.

2. Writing Unit Tests:

Unit tests verify the behavior of individual functions or components. They should be small, fast, and isolated.

```Go
package mypackage

import "testing"

func Add(a, b int) int {
    return a + b
}

func TestAdd(t *testing.T) {
    result := Add(2, 3)
```

```go
    if result != 5 {
        t.Errorf("Add(2, 3) returned %d, expected 5", result)
    }
}

func TestAddNegativeNumbers(t *testing.T) {
    result := Add(-2, -3)
    if result != -5 {
        t.Errorf("Add(-2, -3) returned %d, expected -5", result)
    }
}
```

Run tests using `go test`.

3. Advanced Testing Techniques:

Table-Driven Tests: Useful for testing a function with multiple inputs and expected outputs.

```go
Go
func TestAdd(t *testing.T) {
    testCases := []struct {
        a, b, expected int
    }{
        {2, 3, 5},
        {-2, -3, -5},
        {0, 0, 0},
    }

    for _, tc := range testCases {
        t.Run(fmt.Sprintf("%d+%d", tc.a, tc.b), func(t *testing.T) { //
Subtests for better output
            result := Add(tc.a, tc.b)
            if result != tc.expected {
```

```
            t.Errorf("Add(%d, %d) returned %d, expected %d", tc.a,
tc.b, result, tc.expected)
        }
    })
  }
}
```

Mocking: Isolate units under test by mocking dependencies (network calls, database access, etc.). Consider using a mocking library.

Integration Tests: Test the interaction between multiple components or services.

End-to-End Tests: Test the entire system from the user's perspective.

4. Test Coverage:

Use `go test -cover` to generate test coverage reports. Aim for high test coverage to ensure your code is well-tested.

5. Continuous Integration (CI):

Integrate your tests into a CI pipeline (GitHub Actions, GitLab CI, Jenkins, etc.) to automatically run tests on every code change.

Part 2: Automating Deployment with Go

1. Deployment Strategies:

Blue/Green Deployments: Run two identical environments (blue and green). Deploy the new version to the inactive environment, test it, and then switch traffic.

Canary Deployments: Deploy the new version to a small subset of users or servers (the "canary"). If everything is okay, gradually roll out the deployment to the rest.

Rolling Updates: Update servers or instances one at a time or in batches.

2. Deployment Tools and Techniques:

SSH: For simple deployments, you can use Go's `crypto/ssh` package to connect to remote servers and execute commands.

Cloud Provider APIs: Interact with cloud provider APIs (AWS, GCP, Azure) using their respective Go SDKs.

Kubernetes: Use the Kubernetes API (`k8s.io/client-go`) to deploy and manage applications on Kubernetes clusters.

Configuration Management: Integrate with configuration management tools (Ansible, Chef, Puppet) to automate server configuration.

Containerization (Docker): Build and manage Docker images using Go's Docker client library.

3. Example: Simple SSH Deployment:

Go
```go
package main

import (
    "fmt"
    "log"
    "os/exec"

    "golang.org/x/crypto/ssh"
)
```

```go
func deploy(server, user, binaryPath string) error {
    // ... (SSH client configuration and connection setup - same as
previous examples)

    // Copy the binary using scp
    scpCmd := fmt.Sprintf("scp %s %s@%s:/tmp/", binaryPath,
user, server)
    scp := exec.Command("sh", "-c", scpCmd)
    // ... (Handle scp output and errors)

    // Execute the binary on the remote server
    remoteCmd := fmt.Sprintf("chmod +x /tmp/%s && /tmp/%s",
binaryPath[len(binaryPath)-1], binaryPath[len(binaryPath)-1])
    cmd := fmt.Sprintf("ssh %s@%s '%s'", user, server, remoteCmd)
    // ... (Handle remote command output and errors)

    return nil
}

func main() {
    // ... (Get server, user, binaryPath from config or command-line
args)

    err := deploy(server, user, binaryPath)
    if err != nil {
        log.Fatal(err)
    }

    fmt.Println("Deployment complete.")
}
```

4. Continuous Delivery (CD):

Automate your deployment process as part of a CD pipeline. This allows you to automatically deploy new versions of your application to different environments (development, staging, production) after successful testing.

5. Best Practices:

Infrastructure as Code (IaC): Manage your infrastructure using IaC tools like Terraform.

Version Control: Keep your deployment scripts and configuration files in version control.

Idempotency: Design your deployments to be idempotent, so they can be run multiple times without causing unintended side effects.

Rollback Strategy: Implement a rollback plan to revert to a previous version if the deployment fails.

Monitoring and Logging: Monitor your deployments and applications to detect any issues.

By combining automated testing and deployment with Go, you can create efficient and reliable CI/CD pipelines that streamline the software delivery process. Remember to adapt the examples and best practices to your specific needs and environment.

8.3 Go for CI/CD: Best Practices and Patterns

Go for CI/CD: Best Practices and Patterns

This chapter focuses on best practices and patterns for using Go within Continuous Integration/Continuous Delivery (CI/CD) pipelines. We'll explore how Go's strengths can be leveraged to build robust, efficient, and maintainable CI/CD workflows.

1. Go's Role in CI/CD:

Go excels in various CI/CD stages:

Building: Go's fast compilation makes it ideal for building applications quickly in CI environments.

Testing: Go's built-in testing framework facilitates unit, integration, and end-to-end testing.

Linting & Analysis: Static analysis tools like `golangci-lint` help enforce coding standards and identify potential issues.

Artifact Creation: Go can create deployable artifacts (Docker images, binaries, archives).

Deployment: Go can interact with deployment targets (Kubernetes, cloud providers) via their APIs.

Custom Tooling: Go can create custom tools for pipeline-specific tasks (database migrations, infrastructure setup).

2. CI/CD Pipeline Stages (Example):

A typical Go CI/CD pipeline might include these stages:

Checkout: Retrieve code from version control (Git).

Build: Compile Go code, potentially within a Docker container.

Test: Run unit, integration, and end-to-end tests.

Lint & Analyze: Perform static code analysis.

Build Artifact: Create a deployable artifact (Docker image, binary).

Push Artifact: Upload the artifact to a registry (Docker Hub, cloud registry).

Deploy: Deploy the artifact to the target environment (dev, staging, prod).

Post-Deployment: Run post-deployment checks or tasks.

3. Best Practices and Patterns:

Build Stage:

Docker Multi-Stage Builds: Use multi-stage builds to create small, efficient final images. The build stage compiles the Go application, and a later stage copies only the binary into a minimal base image (e.g., `scratch` or `alpine`).

Caching: Cache Go dependencies (using Go modules' cache) and Docker layers to speed up builds.

Cross-Compilation: Build binaries for different target platforms directly in the CI environment.

Test Stage:

Parallel Testing: Run tests in parallel using `go test -parallel` to reduce testing time

Test Coverage: Aim for high test coverage and use `go test -cover` to generate reports.

Integration Tests: Include integration tests that verify interactions between components. Consider using a testing framework that supports spinning up external dependencies (databases, message queues) for the tests.

End-to-End Tests: Implement end-to-end tests to validate the entire application flow.

Lint & Analyze Stage:

`golangci-lint`: Use `golangci-lint` for comprehensive static analysis. Configure it to match your project's coding style.

Fail on Lint Errors: Treat linting errors as build failures to enforce code quality.

Build Artifact Stage:

Docker Images: Build Docker images for containerized deployments.

Version Tagging: Tag artifacts (images, binaries) with version numbers, commit hashes, or build IDs for traceability.

Push Artifact Stage:

Docker Registries: Push Docker images to a registry (Docker Hub, ECR, GCR, ACR).

Authentication: Securely manage registry credentials using CI/CD secrets.

Deploy Stage:

Kubernetes Deployments: Use `kubectl` or the Kubernetes Go client to deploy to Kubernetes.

Cloud Provider Deployments: Use cloud provider SDKs to deploy to cloud services (AWS ECS, Google Cloud Run, Azure App Service).

Infrastructure as Code (IaC): Manage infrastructure with Terraform or similar tools. Integrate IaC deployments into the pipeline.

Deployment Strategies: Implement blue/green, canary, or rolling update deployments.

General CI/CD Best Practices:

Idempotency: Design your deployments to be idempotent.

Rollback Strategy: Have a clear rollback plan in case of failed deployments.

Monitoring & Logging: Integrate with monitoring and logging systems.

Security: Secure your CI/CD pipeline and protect credentials.

Pipeline as Code: Define your CI/CD pipeline as code (YAML, JSON) for version control and reproducibility.

4. Example: GitHub Actions Workflow Snippet:

```yaml
YAML
jobs:
  build:
    runs-on: ubuntu-latest
    steps:
      - uses: actions/checkout@v3
      - uses: actions/setup-go@v3
        with:
          go-version: '^1.20'
      - run: go build -o myapp ./...
      - run: go test -v ./... -coverprofile=coverage.out
      - run: golangci-lint run
      - name: Build Docker Image
        run: docker build -t my-go-image:latest .
      - name: Push Docker Image
        run: |
```

```
        docker login -u ${{ secrets.DOCKER_USERNAME }} -p ${{
secrets.DOCKER_PASSWORD }}
        docker push my-go-image:latest
  deploy:
    needs: build
    runs-on: ubuntu-latest
    steps:
      - uses: actions/checkout@v3
      - uses: azure/setup-kubectl@v2
        with:
          version: v1.27.3
      - run: kubectl apply -f deployment.yaml
```

5. Go Tooling for CI/CD:

`go build`: Compiles Go code.

`go test`: Runs tests.

`golangci-lint`: Linter.

`gox`: Cross-compilation tool.

`goreleaser`: Release automation tool.

By following these best practices and leveraging Go's capabilities, you can build robust and efficient CI/CD pipelines for your Go applications. Remember to adapt these patterns to your specific CI/CD tool and project requirements. This chapter provides a strong foundation for building effective CI/CD workflows with Go.

Chapter 9

Monitoring and Logging with Go

9.1 Collecting and Analyzing Metrics with Go

This chapter explores collecting and analyzing metrics using Go. We'll cover instrumenting your Go applications to expose metrics, using Prometheus to collect and store these metrics, and visualizing the data with Grafana.

1. Instrumenting Your Go Application:

The first step is to instrument your Go application to collect metrics. The most popular way to do this is with the Prometheus client library for Go (github.com/prometheus/client_golang).

Go
package main

```
import (
    "net/http"
    "time"

    "github.com/prometheus/client_golang/prometheus"
    "github.com/prometheus/client_golang/prometheus/promhttp"
)

var (
    httpRequestsTotal = prometheus.NewCounterVec(
        prometheus.CounterOpts{
            Name: "http_requests_total",
            Help: "Total number of HTTP requests.",
```

```go
    },
    []string{"method", "path"},
  )

  httpRequestLatency = prometheus.NewHistogramVec(
    prometheus.HistogramOpts{
      Name:   "http_request_latency_seconds",
      Help:   "Latency of HTTP requests.",
        Buckets: []float64{0.001, 0.005, 0.01, 0.025, 0.05, 0.1,
0.25, 0.5, 1}, // Example buckets
    },
    []string{"method", "path"},
  )
)

func init() {
  // Register metrics with Prometheus
  prometheus.MustRegister(httpRequestsTotal)
  prometheus.MustRegister(httpRequestLatency)
}

func myHandler(w http.ResponseWriter, r *http.Request) {
  start := time.Now()
  // ... Your request handling logic ...
  timeTaken := time.Since(start).Seconds()

   httpRequestsTotal.With(prometheus.Labels{"method": r.Method,
"path": r.URL.Path}).Inc()
          httpRequestLatency.With(prometheus.Labels{"method":
r.Method, "path": r.URL.Path}).Observe(timeTaken)

  fmt.Fprintln(w, "Hello, Prometheus!")
}

func main() {
```

```
    http.HandleFunc("/", myHandler)
    http.Handle("/metrics", promhttp.Handler()) // Expose metrics
endpoint

    http.ListenAndServe(":8080", nil)
}
```

Explanation:

`httpRequestsTotal`: A counter to track the total number of HTTP requests. `CounterVec` allows you to add labels (method, path) to distinguish between different requests.

`httpRequestLatency`: A histogram to track the latency of HTTP requests. Histograms provide buckets to see the distribution of latencies.

`prometheus.MustRegister`: Registers the metrics with Prometheus so they can be scraped.

The handler increments the counter and observes the latency for each request.

`/metrics` endpoint: Exposes the metrics in a format Prometheus can understand.

2. Running Prometheus:

Download and run Prometheus. Configure it to scrape your application's `/metrics` endpoint. A simple `prometheus.yml` configuration:

```yaml
YAML
global:
  scrape_interval:    15s # Scrape every 15 seconds
```

```
scrape_configs:
  - job_name: 'my-go-app'
    static_configs:
      - targets: ['localhost:8080']
```

3. Visualizing Metrics with Grafana:

Download and run Grafana. Configure a Prometheus data source pointing to your Prometheus server. You can then create dashboards in Grafana to visualize your metrics. Grafana can query Prometheus and display the data in various formats (graphs, tables, gauges).

4. Key Metrics to Collect:

Request Rate: How many requests your application is handling per second.

Latency: How long it takes to process requests.

Error Rate: The percentage of requests that result in errors.

Resource Usage: CPU, memory, and disk usage.

Custom Application Metrics: Metrics specific to your application's logic (e.g., number of users, items processed).

5. Advanced Metrics:

Gauges: Track current values (e.g., number of active users).

Histograms: Track the distribution of values (e.g., request latency).

Summaries: Similar to histograms but also provide quantiles.

6. Best Practices:

Meaningful Metric Names: Use descriptive metric names.

Labels: Use labels to add dimensions to your metrics.

Consistent Units: Use consistent units for your metrics (e.g., seconds for latency).

Alerting: Set up alerts in Prometheus or Grafana to be notified when important metrics cross thresholds.

By instrumenting your Go applications with Prometheus and visualizing the metrics with Grafana, you can gain valuable insights into your application's performance and identify potential issues. This chapter provides a solid foundation for collecting and analyzing metrics in your Go applications. Remember to install the Prometheus client library using `go get github.com/prometheus/client_golang/prometheus` and `go get github.com/prometheus/client_golang/promhttp`.

9.2 Building Monitoring Agents and Dashboards in Go

This chapter explores building monitoring agents and dashboards in Go. We'll cover collecting system metrics, application metrics, and logs, and then visualizing this data in custom dashboards.

1. Building Monitoring Agents:

Monitoring agents are responsible for collecting data from various sources. Go is well-suited for building these agents due to its concurrency, networking capabilities, and ease of use.

1.1. Collecting System Metrics:

Go provides access to system information through packages like `runtime`, `os`, and `syscall`. You can also use third-party libraries for more detailed metrics.

Go

```go
package main

import (
    "fmt"
    "log"
    "runtime"
    "time"

    "github.com/shirou/gopsutil/cpu" // Example: gopsutil for CPU metrics
    "github.com/shirou/gopsutil/mem"
)

func main() {
    for range time.Tick(time.Second) { // Collect metrics every second
        memInfo, err := mem.VirtualMemory()
        if err != nil {
            log.Println("Error getting memory info:", err)
        }

        cpuPercent, err := cpu.Percent(time.Second, false) // Non-blocking CPU usage
        if err != nil {
            log.Println("Error getting CPU usage:", err)
        }

        fmt.Printf("CPU: %.1f%%, Memory: %.1f%% (%.1f GB total, %.1f GB available)\n",
```

```
            cpuPercent[0],
            (1-memInfo.AvailablePercent)*100, // Memory used
percentage
        float64(memInfo.Total)/1024/1024/1024,
        float64(memInfo.Available)/1024/1024/1024,
            )


    // More system metrics (disk, network, etc.) using gopsutil or
other libraries.
    // Example using runtime package for goroutines
                    fmt.Printf("Number of Goroutines: %d\n",
runtime.NumGoroutine())


    }
}
```

1.2. Collecting Application Metrics:

Instrument your application to expose metrics (as covered in the previous chapter). Agents can then collect these metrics. Prometheus is a common tool for this.

1.3. Collecting Logs:

Agents can collect logs from various sources (files, syslog, etc.) and forward them to a central logging system (e.g., Elasticsearch, Loki). Consider using a log shipper like Fluentd or Filebeat, or write a custom one in Go.

2. Building Dashboards:

You can build custom dashboards to visualize the collected data. Several options exist:

Grafana: A popular open-source dashboarding tool that integrates well with Prometheus and other data sources.

Custom Web UI: Build your own web UI using Go's `net/http` package and a frontend framework (React, Vue, etc.).

Termdash: For simple terminal based dashboards.

2.1. Example: Building a Simple Web Dashboard (Conceptual):

```go
package main

import (
    "fmt"
    "net/http"
    "time"
    // ... (Import your metrics collection functions)
)

func dashboardHandler(w http.ResponseWriter, r *http.Request) {
    // Get the latest metrics
    cpuPercent := getCPUUsage()
    memPercent := getMemoryUsage()
    // ... (Get other metrics)

    // Generate HTML dynamically (or use a templating engine)
    fmt.Fprintf(w, `
<html>
<head><title>System Dashboard</title></head>
<body>
<h1>System Metrics</h1>
<p>CPU Usage: %.1f%%</p>
<p>Memory Usage: %.1f%%</p>
// ... (Display other metrics)
```

```
</body>
</html>`, cpuPercent, memPercent)
}

func main() {
    http.HandleFunc("/", dashboardHandler)
    fmt.Println("Dashboard listening on :8080")
    log.Fatal(http.ListenAndServe(":8080", nil))
}
```

3. Data Storage and Processing:

Time-Series Databases: For metrics, time-series databases like Prometheus, InfluxDB, or TimesDB are ideal.

Logging Systems: For logs, Elasticsearch, Loki, or cloud-provider logging services are common choices.

Message Queues: For high-volume data streams, message queues like Kafka or RabbitMQ can buffer data before processing.

4. Best Practices:

Modular Design: Design your agents and dashboards in a modular way to make them easier to maintain and extend.

Configuration: Use configuration files or environment variables to manage agent and dashboard settings.

Error Handling: Implement robust error handling to prevent your agents from crashing.

Security: Securely manage access to your monitoring data and dashboards.

Alerting: Set up alerts to be notified when important metrics cross thresholds.

Building monitoring agents and dashboards allows you to gain valuable insights into the health and performance of your systems and applications. Go's versatility makes it a great choice for building these essential tools. Remember to install any required Go packages using `go get`. This chapter provides a solid foundation; consult the documentation for the specific libraries and tools you use for more advanced features.

9.3 Go for Observability: Logs, Metrics, and Tracing

This chapter explores using Go for observability, covering logs, metrics, and tracing. These three pillars are crucial for understanding the behavior of your applications in production, especially in complex distributed systems.

1. Logging:

Structured logging is essential for easy log analysis. Libraries like `logrus` and `zap` provide structured logging capabilities in Go.

```Go
package main

import (
    "context"
    "os"

    "github.com/sirupsen/logrus" // Or use "go.uber.org/zap" for more performance
)
```

```go
func main() {
    // Logrus example
    log := logrus.New()
        log.SetFormatter(&logrus.JSONFormatter{}) // Use JSON
format for structured logs
    log.SetOutput(os.Stdout)

  // Add fields to the log entry
    ctx := context.Background() // You might get this from the
request context
    logEntry := log.WithFields(logrus.Fields{
    "component": "my-service",
    "request_id": "12345", // Example: Add a request ID
        "user_id": "67890",
  }).WithContext(ctx)

    logEntry.Info("Starting application...")
    logEntry.Warn("A warning occurred.")
    logEntry.Error("An error occurred.")

    //Zap Example
    // logger, _ := zap.NewProduction()
    // defer logger.Sync() // flushes buffer, if any
    // sugar := logger.Sugar()
    // sugar.Infow("failed to fetch URL",
    //      "url", "http://example.com",
    //      "attempt", 3,
    // )
    // sugar.Errorw("failed to fetch URL",
    //      "url", "http://example.com",
    //      "attempt", 3,
    //      "error", err,
    // )
}
```

Best Practices for Logging:

Structured Logs: Use JSON or other structured formats.

Contextual Information: Include relevant information (request ID, user ID) in log entries.

Log Levels: Use appropriate log levels (debug, info, warn, error, fatal).

Centralized Logging: Aggregate logs from all your services in a central location (e.g., Elasticsearch, Loki).

2. Metrics:

Metrics provide insights into the performance and health of your applications. Prometheus is a popular choice for collecting and visualizing metrics.

Go
```go
package main

import (
    "net/http"

    "github.com/prometheus/client_golang/prometheus"
    "github.com/prometheus/client_golang/prometheus/promhttp"
)

var (
    httpRequestsTotal = prometheus.NewCounterVec(
        prometheus.CounterOpts{
            Name: "http_requests_total",
            Help: "Total number of HTTP requests.",
        },
```

```go
        []string{"method", "path"},
    )
)

func init() {
    prometheus.MustRegister(httpRequestsTotal)
}

func myHandler(w http.ResponseWriter, r *http.Request) {
        httpRequestsTotal.With(prometheus.Labels{"method":
r.Method, "path": r.URL.Path}).Inc()
    // ... Your handler logic ...
}

func main() {
    http.HandleFunc("/", myHandler)
     http.Handle("/metrics", promhttp.Handler()) // Expose metrics
endpoint
    http.ListenAndServe(":8080", nil)
}
```

Best Practices for Metrics:

Meaningful Metrics: Collect metrics that are relevant to your application's performance.

Labels: Use labels to add dimensions to your metrics.

Histograms and Summaries: Use histograms and summaries to track distributions of values (e.g., request latency).

Alerting: Set up alerts based on your metrics.

3. Tracing:

Distributed tracing helps you understand how requests propagate through your distributed system. OpenTelemetry is a popular open-source framework for tracing.

```go
Go
package main

import (
    "context"
    "go.opentelemetry.io/otel"

"go.opentelemetry.io/otel/exporters/otlp/otlptrace/otlptracegrpc"
    "go.opentelemetry.io/otel/propagation"
    "go.opentelemetry.io/otel/sdk/resource"
    sdktrace "go.opentelemetry.io/otel/sdk/trace"
    semconv "go.opentelemetry.io/otel/semconv/v1.4.0"
    "google.golang.org/grpc"
    "log"
)

func initTracer() (*sdktrace.TracerProvider, error) {
    ctx := context.Background()

    res, err := resource.New(ctx,
        resource.WithAttributes(
                // the service name used to display traces in
backends
                semconv.ServiceNameKey.String("my-go-service"),
        ),
    )
    if err != nil {
            return nil, fmt.Errorf("failed to create resource: %w", err)
    }
```

```go
// Set up a trace exporter
ctx, cancel := context.WithTimeout(ctx, time.Second)
defer cancel()
        conn, err := grpc.DialContext(ctx, "localhost:4317",
grpc.WithBlock(), grpc.WithInsecure()) // Replace with your
collector address
if err != nil {
        return nil, fmt.Errorf("failed to create gRPC connection to
collector: %w", err)
}

exporter, err := otlptracegrpc.New(ctx,
        otlptracegrpc.WithGRPCConn(conn),
        otlptracegrpc.WithRetry(otlptracegrpc.RetryConfig{
                InitialInterval: time.Second,
                MaxInterval:    time.Second * 60,
                MaxAttempts:    20,
        }),
)

if err != nil {
        return nil, fmt.Errorf("failed to create trace exporter: %w",
err)
}

// Register the trace exporter with a TracerProvider, using a
deterministic sampling policy
tp := sdktrace.NewTracerProvider(
        sdktrace.WithBatcher(exporter),
        sdktrace.WithResource(res),
)
otel.SetTracerProvider(tp)

otel.SetTextMapPropagator(propagation.NewCompositeTextMapPr
opagator(propagation.TraceContext{}, propagation.Baggage{}))
```

```go
        return tp, nil
}

func main() {
        tp, err := initTracer()
    if err != nil {
        log.Fatal(err)
    }
    defer func() {
        if err := tp.Shutdown(context.Background()); err != nil {
            log.Printf("Error shutting down tracer provider: %v", err)
        }
    }()

    ctx := context.Background()
    tr := otel.Tracer("my-instrumentation-library-name")

    ctx, span := tr.Start(ctx, "my-span-name")
    defer span.End()

        // ... Your application logic, instrumented with spans ...

}
```

Best Practices for Tracing:

Span Context: Propagate span context across service boundaries.

Meaningful Span Names: Use descriptive span names.

Tags: Add tags to spans to provide additional context.

Sampling: Use sampling to reduce the volume of trace data.

Tools and Libraries:

Logging: `logrus`, `zap`

Metrics: `github.com/prometheus/client_golang`

Tracing: `go.opentelemetry.io/otel`

By combining logging, metrics, and tracing, you can gain a comprehensive understanding of your Go applications' behavior and performance. This allows you to identify and resolve issues quickly, optimize performance, and ensure the reliability of your systems. Remember to install the required Go packages using `go get`. This chapter provides a solid foundation for observability in Go; refer to the documentation for the specific libraries and tools you are using for more advanced features.

Chapter 10

Security Best Practices in Go for DevOps

10.1 Securing Your Go DevOps Applications

Securing your Go DevOps applications is paramount. This chapter covers crucial security best practices and patterns to protect your applications and infrastructure.

1. Input Validation:

Sanitize all user input: Never trust user input. Validate and sanitize all data received from users (forms, APIs, command-line arguments) to prevent injection attacks (SQL injection, cross-site scripting (XSS), command injection).

Use parameterized queries: When interacting with databases, always use parameterized queries or prepared statements to prevent SQL injection.

Validate data types and formats: Ensure that input data matches the expected data types and formats.

Regular expressions (with caution): Use regular expressions for complex input validation, but be mindful of ReDoS (Regular Expression Denial of Service) attacks. Keep your regexes simple and test their performance.

2. Authentication and Authorization:

Use strong authentication methods: Implement strong authentication mechanisms (e.g., multi-factor authentication

(MFA), OAuth 2.0) to verify user identities. Avoid storing passwords directly; hash them using bcrypt or Argon2.

Principle of Least Privilege: Grant users and services only the necessary permissions.

Role-Based Access Control (RBAC): Implement RBAC to manage user permissions based on their roles.

Secure API keys: Protect API keys and treat them as sensitive information. Store them securely (environment variables, secrets management systems). Use short-lived API keys if possible.

JWT (JSON Web Tokens): Use JWTs for stateless authentication and authorization in APIs.

3. Data Protection:

Encrypt sensitive data at rest: Encrypt sensitive data stored in databases or files.

Encrypt data in transit: Use HTTPS to encrypt communication between clients and your application. Ensure that your TLS configuration is strong (disable weak ciphers).

Use HTTPS for internal communication: Encrypt communication between internal services as well.

Protect against data breaches: Implement measures to detect and respond to data breaches.

4. Secure Coding Practices:

Avoid unsafe functions: Be cautious when using unsafe functions in Go. Understand the potential risks.

Handle errors gracefully: Don't expose sensitive information in error messages. Log errors for debugging but return generic error messages to users.

Keep dependencies updated: Regularly update your Go dependencies to patch security vulnerabilities. Use `go mod tidy` and `go mod vendor`.

Code reviews: Conduct regular code reviews to identify security vulnerabilities.

Static analysis: Use static analysis tools (e.g., `golangci-lint`, `govulncheck`) to detect potential security issues in your code.

5. Infrastructure Security:

Secure your servers: Harden your servers by disabling unnecessary services and using strong passwords.

Firewall configuration: Configure firewalls to restrict access to your servers

Regular security audits: Conduct regular security audits to identify vulnerabilities.

Intrusion Detection/Prevention Systems (IDS/IPS): Use IDS/IPS to detect and prevent malicious activity.

Container security: If using Docker, follow Docker security best practices. Use minimal base images, run containers as non-root users, and scan images for vulnerabilities.

Kubernetes security: If deploying to Kubernetes, follow Kubernetes security best practices. Use RBAC, network policies, and security contexts.

6. Secrets Management:

Never hardcode secrets: Never hardcode API keys, passwords, or other sensitive information in your code.

Environment variables: Use environment variables for configuration, but avoid storing sensitive information directly in them.

Secrets management systems: Use dedicated secrets management systems (HashiCorp Vault, AWS Secrets Manager, Google Cloud Secret Manager, Azure Key Vault) to store and manage sensitive information.

7. Dependency Management:

Vendoring dependencies: Vendor your dependencies to ensure that you are using known versions.

Dependency scanning: Use tools to scan your dependencies for known vulnerabilities.

8. Security Auditing:

Regular penetration testing: Conduct regular penetration testing to identify vulnerabilities in your applications and infrastructure.

Security scanning tools: Use automated security scanning tools to identify vulnerabilities.

9. Denial-of-Service (DoS) Protection:

Rate limiting: Implement rate limiting to prevent abuse of your APIs.

Traffic shaping: Use traffic shaping to manage network traffic and prevent DoS attacks.

Cloud provider protections: Leverage cloud provider DDoS protection services.

10. Secure Deployment Practices:

Immutable infrastructure: Deploy new versions of your application instead of modifying existing ones.

Automated deployments: Automate your deployments to reduce the risk of human error.

11. Incident Response Plan:

Have a plan: Develop an incident response plan to handle security incidents.

Regularly test your plan: Regularly test your incident response plan to ensure it is effective.

By following these security best practices, you can significantly improve the security posture of your Go DevOps applications. Security is an ongoing process, so it's important to stay up-to-date with the latest security threats and best practices.

10.2 Implementing Security Automation with Go

Implementing security automation with Go allows you to proactively address security concerns, reduce manual effort, and improve the overall security posture of your applications and infrastructure. Go's capabilities in systems programming, networking, and concurrency make it well-suited for building security automation tools.

1. Common Security Automation Tasks:

Vulnerability Scanning: Automate vulnerability scanning of your applications and infrastructure using tools like OpenVAS, Nessus, or custom scripts.

Security Hardening: Automate the process of hardening servers and applications by applying security configurations and patches.

Compliance Checking: Automate checks to ensure compliance with security policies and regulations (e.g., PCI DSS, HIPAA).

Incident Response: Automate parts of the incident response process, such as isolating affected systems or collecting forensic data.

Log Analysis: Automate the analysis of logs to detect suspicious activity.

Security Testing: Automate security testing, including penetration testing and fuzzing.

Threat Intelligence: Integrate with threat intelligence feeds to automatically identify and respond to potential threats.

Cloud Security Automation: Automate security tasks in cloud environments, such as configuring security groups, managing IAM roles, and monitoring cloud resources.

2. Using Go for Security Automation:

Go can be used to build various security automation tools:

Custom Scripts: Write Go scripts to automate specific security tasks, such as checking file integrity, scanning for open ports, or enforcing password policies.

Security Tools: Develop full-fledged security tools in Go, such as vulnerability scanners, intrusion detection systems, or security auditing tools.

Integration with Security Tools: Use Go to integrate with existing security tools and APIs.

Kubernetes Operators: Build Kubernetes operators to automate security tasks in Kubernetes environments.

3. Example: Automating Vulnerability Scanning with Go:

Go
```go
package main

import (
    "fmt"
    "log"
    "os/exec"
)

func scanVulnerabilities(target string) (string, error) {
    // Example using OpenVAS (replace with your preferred tool)
    cmd := exec.Command("openvas-scan", "--target", target) // Adjust command as needed
    output, err := cmd.CombinedOutput()
    if err != nil {
        return "", fmt.Errorf("vulnerability scan failed: %w\nOutput: %s", err, output)
    }
    return string(output), nil
}

func main() {
    target := "192.168.1.100" // Replace with your target
    report, err := scanVulnerabilities(target)
```

```go
    if err != nil {
        log.Fatal(err)
    }

    fmt.Println(report)

    // Example: Parse the report and take action (e.g., create a
ticket, notify admin)
}
```

4. Example: Automating Security Hardening with Go and SSH:

```go
Go
package main

import (
    "fmt"
    "log"
    "os/exec"

    "golang.org/x/crypto/ssh"
)

func hardenServer(server, user string) error {
    config := &ssh.ClientConfig{
        User: user,
            Auth: &ssh.Password("yourpassword"), // In real-world,
use key-based auth
                HostKeyCallback: ssh.InsecureIgnoreHostKey(), //
Insecure for demo, use proper host key verification
    }
    client, err := ssh.Dial("tcp", server+":22", config)
    if err != nil {
        return fmt.Errorf("dial failed: %w", err)
```

```go
	}
	defer client.Close()

	session, err := client.NewSession()
	if err != nil {
		return fmt.Errorf("session failed: %w", err)
	}
	defer session.Close()

	commands := []string{
		"apt-get update", // Example: Update package lists
		"apt-get upgrade -y", // Example: Upgrade packages
		// ... Add more hardening commands ...
	}

	for _, cmd := range commands {
		output, err := session.CombinedOutput([]byte(cmd))
		if err != nil {
			return fmt.Errorf("command '%s' failed: %w\nOutput: %s", cmd, err, output)
		}
		fmt.Println(string(output))
	}

	return nil
}

func main() {
	server := "yourserver"
	user := "youruser"

	err := hardenServer(server, user)
	if err != nil {
		log.Fatal(err)
	}
```

```
    fmt.Println("Server hardening complete.")
}
```

5. Best Practices:

Modular Design: Design your security automation tools in a modular way to make them easier to maintain and extend.

Configuration: Use configuration files or environment variables to manage settings.

Error Handling: Implement robust error handling.

Logging: Log all security-related events.

Testing: Thoroughly test your security automation tools.

Security: Securely manage credentials and access to your systems.

Version Control: Keep your security automation scripts and tools in version control.

By automating security tasks with Go, you can improve the efficiency and effectiveness of your security operations. Go's flexibility and performance make it a valuable tool for building security automation solutions. Remember to install any required Go packages using `go get`. This chapter provides a solid foundation; consult the documentation for specific tools and libraries for more advanced details.

10.3 Go for DevSecOps: Building Secure Cloud-Native Systems

Go is an excellent language for building secure cloud-native systems within a DevSecOps framework. Its performance, concurrency, and strong standard library make it well-suited for developing secure and reliable applications in modern distributed environments.

1. DevSecOps Principles and Go's Role:

DevSecOps emphasizes integrating security throughout the software development lifecycle, from design to deployment and operations. Go plays a crucial role in implementing DevSecOps practices:

Shift-Left Security: Go's static analysis tools (e.g., `golangci-lint`, `govulncheck`) help identify security vulnerabilities early in the development process. This "shift-left" approach reduces the cost and effort of fixing security issues later.

Automated Security Testing: Go's testing framework can be used to automate security tests, such as unit tests for security-related functions, integration tests to verify secure interactions between components, and end-to-end tests to simulate real-world attacks.

Secure Coding Practices: Go's strong type system and memory safety features help prevent common security vulnerabilities. Following secure coding guidelines and best practices when writing Go code is essential.

Infrastructure as Code (IaC) Security: Go can be used to build tools that automate security checks for IaC configurations (Terraform, CloudFormation).

Security Automation: Go can be used to automate various security tasks, such as vulnerability scanning, security hardening, compliance checking, and incident response.

Cloud-Native Security: Go is well-suited for building cloud-native security tools and services that integrate with Kubernetes and other cloud platforms.

2. Secure Coding Practices in Go:

Input Validation: Sanitize all user input to prevent injection attacks. Use parameterized queries for database interactions.

Error Handling: Handle errors gracefully and avoid exposing sensitive information in error messages.

Authentication and Authorization: Use strong authentication methods (MFA, OAuth 2.0) and implement least privilege and RBAC.

Data Protection: Encrypt sensitive data at rest and in transit.

Secrets Management: Use a secrets management system (HashiCorp Vault, cloud provider secrets managers) to store and manage sensitive information.

Dependency Management: Keep dependencies updated and scan them for vulnerabilities. Use `go mod tidy` and `go mod vendor`. Use `govulncheck` regularly.

Static Analysis: Use static analysis tools to identify potential security issues in your code.

Code Reviews: Conduct regular code reviews with a focus on security.

3. Automating Security Testing with Go:

Go
```go
package main

import (
    "testing"
    // ... (Import your security testing libraries or functions)
)

func TestXSSPrevention(t *testing.T) {
        // Example: Test for XSS vulnerability in a function that renders user input
    userInput := "<script>alert('XSS')</script>"
     expectedOutput := "&lt;script&gt;alert('XSS')&lt;/script&gt;" // HTML-encoded output

            actualOutput := sanitizeUserInput(userInput) // Your sanitization function

    if actualOutput != expectedOutput {
            t.Errorf("XSS vulnerability not prevented. Expected: %s, Got: %s", expectedOutput, actualOutput)
    }
}

// ... (More security tests for SQL injection, command injection, etc.)
```

4. Building Security Automation Tools with Go:

Go can be used to build various security automation tools:

Vulnerability Scanners: Integrate with existing vulnerability scanning tools or write custom scanners.

Security Hardening Tools: Automate the process of applying security configurations and patches.

Compliance Checking Tools: Automate checks to ensure compliance with security policies.

Incident Response Tools: Automate parts of the incident response process.

5. Go for Cloud-Native Security:

Kubernetes Security: Go is commonly used to develop Kubernetes controllers and operators that automate security tasks in Kubernetes environments.

Cloud Provider Security: Use cloud provider Go SDKs to automate security tasks in cloud environments.

Service Mesh Security: Integrate with service meshes (Istio, Linkerd) for secure communication between services.

6. DevSecOps Pipeline Integration:

Integrate security tools and checks into your CI/CD pipeline. This ensures that security is considered at every stage of the software development lifecycle.

7. Best Practices for Go DevSecOps:

Security Training: Provide security training to developers and operations teams.

Threat Modeling: Conduct threat modeling exercises to identify potential security risks.

Security Champions: Designate security champions within development teams to promote security awareness.

Regular Security Audits: Conduct regular security audits and penetration testing.

Incident Response Plan: Have a well-defined incident response plan in place.

Continuous Improvement: Continuously improve your security practices based on lessons learned and new threats.

By adopting a DevSecOps approach and leveraging Go's capabilities, you can build secure and resilient cloud-native systems. Remember that security is an ongoing process and requires continuous effort and vigilance. This chapter provides a strong foundation for building secure systems with Go; always refer to the latest security best practices and guidelines.